Communications in Computer and Information Science 1106

Commenced Publication in 2007
Founding and Former Series Editors:
Phoebe Chen, Alfredo Cuzzocrea, Xiaoyong Du, Orhun Kara, Ting Liu,
Krishna M. Sivalingam, Dominik Ślęzak, Takashi Washio, Xiaokang Yang,
and Junsong Yuan

More information about this series at http://www.springer.com/series/7899

Paulo Meirelles · Maria Augusta Nelson ·
Carla Rocha (Eds.)

Agile Methods

10th Brazilian Workshop, WBMA 2019
Belo Horizonte, Brazil, September 11, 2019
Revised Selected Papers

 Springer

Editors
Paulo Meirelles (iD)
Federal University of São Paulo
São Paulo, Brazil

Carla Rocha (iD)
University of Brasília
Brasília, Brazil

Maria Augusta Nelson (iD)
Pontifical Catholic University
of Minas Gerais
Belo Horizonte, Brazil

ISSN 1865-0929   ISSN 1865-0937 (electronic)
Communications in Computer and Information Science
ISBN 978-3-030-36700-8   ISBN 978-3-030-36701-5 (eBook)
https://doi.org/10.1007/978-3-030-36701-5

This Springer imprint is published by the registered company Springer Nature Switzerland AG
The registered company address is: Gewerbestrasse 11, 6330 Cham, Switzerland

Preface

Welcome to the 10th edition of the Brazilian Workshop on Agile Methods (WBMA 2019) held in Belo Horizonte, Minas Gerais, Brazil, on September 11, 2019. WBMA is the research track in the Agile Brazil conference. It is an academic event that focuses on agile software development. This year's edition comes with a history of successes. The workshop has been a reference point for the Brazilian research community in Agile Methods for ten years, promoting research activities in the area.

All of the submitted papers (research, experience reports, non-systematic literature reviews, and position papers) went through a rigorous peer-review process. At least three members of the Program Committee reviewed each paper. Of the 21 papers submitted, only 6 were accepted as full papers (28.5%). We also accepted four experience reports. The Program Committee evaluated each report submission for new experiences that would be both interesting and beneficial to the Brazilian Agile Methods community. In summary, we accepted papers dealing with three different aspects of Agile Methods, such as Agile in education, empirical studies on Agile, and Agile practices.

Moreover, as a special edition celebrating ten years of the workshop, we had two invited papers. The first one is a position paper by Claudia Melo, the WBMA 2019 Award Chair. She presents a short narrative on what has been the need for agility, its evolution, and a possible re-purpose based on our global sustainable development challenges. Another invited work is a full paper by Alfredo Goldman, who was awarded, given several criteria analyzed by the WBMA 2019 Chairs, the Most influential Researcher over ten years of WBMA. He reports his "fun journey" researching Agile Methods, summarizing almost two decades of research on Agile Methods. He shows the influence of his work within Agile Methods since 2001, not only on teaching but also on the research field and on the Brazilian software development industry.

We hope that you will find the WBMA 2019 proceedings useful for your educational, professional, and academic activities.

Finally, we would like to thank all the people who contributed to WBMA 2019, including the authors, reviewers, volunteers, and the previous and current chairs. A special thanks to the Agile Brazil conference organizers for their support and partnership.

September 2019

Paulo Meirelles
Maria Augusta Nelson
Carla Rocha

Organization

Program Committee

Ademar Aguiar	Faculty of Engineering of the University of Porto, Portugal
Adolfo Neto	Universidade Tecnológica Federal do Paraná, Brazil
Alfredo Goldman	Universidade de São Paulo, Brazil
André Duarte	Instituto Federal do Rio Grande do Norte, Brazil
Anh Nguyen	University College of Southeast Norway, Norway
Carla Rocha	Universidade de Brasília, Brazil
Christina Von Flach	Universidade Federal da Bahia, Brazil
Claudia Melo	Universidade de Brasília, Brazil
Eduardo Figueiredo	Universidade Federal de Minas Gerais, Brazil
Eduardo Guerra	National Institute of Space Research, Brazil
Fabio Kon	Universidade de São Paulo, Brazil
Fábio Levy Siqueira	POLI-USP, Brazil
Felipe Furtado	CESAR, Brazil
Filipe Correia	Faculty of Engineering of the University of Porto, Portugal
Genaina Rodrigues	Universidade de Brasília, Brazil
Graziela Tonin	Universidade Federal da Fronteira Sul, Brazil
Gregorio Robles	Universidad Rey Juan Carlos, Spain
Heitor Augustus	Universidade Federal de Lavras, Brazil
Hilmer Neri	Universidade de Brasília, Brazil
Jutta Eckstein	IT Communication, Germany
Kecia Ferreira	Instituto Federal de Minas Gerais, Brazil
Maarit Laanti	Nitor Delta, Finland
Marcelo Maia	Universidade Federal de Uberlândia, Brazil
Marcelo Pimenta	Universidade Federal do Rio Grande do Sul, Brazil
Marcelo Werneck	PUC-MG, Brazil
Marco Túlio Valente	Universidade Federal de Minas Gerais, Brazil
Renato Coral	Universidade de Brasília, Brazil
Ricardo Terra	Universidade Federal de Lavras, Brazil
Rodrigo Santos	UniRio, Brazil
Tiago Silva Da Silva	Universidade Federal de São Paulo, Brazil
Xiaofeng Wang	Free University of Bozen-Bolzano, Italy

Co-reviewers

Adriano Lages dos Santos	Universidade Federal de Minas Gerais, Brazil
Awdren Fontão	SIDIA Instituto de Ciência e Tecnologia, Brazil
Diogo Pina	Universidade de São Paulo, Brazil
Jailton Coelho	Universidade Federal de Minas Gerais, Brazil
Johnatan Oliveira	Universidade Federal de Minas Gerais, Brazil
Luciana Silva	Universidade Federal de Minas Gerais, Brazil
Thatiane Rosa	Universidade de São Paulo and Instituto Federal do Tocantins, Brazil

Contents

Agile Practices

**A Closing Paper From the Most Influential Researcher
Over 10 Years of WBMA**

An Opening Paper From the Award Chair

Another Purpose for Agility: Sustainability

Claudia de O. Melo[✉]

International Atomic Energy Agency, Vienna, Austria
c.melo@iaea.org
http://www.iaea.org

Abstract. This position paper aims at building a short narrative on what has been the need for agility, its evolution, and a possible re-purpose based on our global sustainable development challenges. Agile implies that a software development team (or now entire organizations) should be resilient, adaptable, and quickly learn, which is also a great capability featured by nature. However, the justification for becoming agile is being a chorus of voices repeating the same mantra: competitive advantage. The evolution of agility could be shaped by forces of cooperation, instead of only of competition, with a purpose to enable a better and more sustainable future for society. There is a strong case for inter- and trans-disciplinarity in agile, technology and sustainable development research, where agility has definitely a role.

Keywords: ICT4S · Agility · Sustainability

1 The Need for Agility

Agile has an important role in the current technological revolution, as it enables technologists to quickly adapt and evolve the digital systems that are transforming our economy and society. The Digital Economy is considered the single most important driver of innovation in countries [3], with a promise to contribute to inclusion, sustainability and peace [11].

When reflecting on the origins of agility, there was a combination of factors fostering agile ideas. Mostly a **reaction** to heavyweight, prescriptive approaches to software development, combined to the **increasing level of change** in the business environment urged practitioners to **handle complex and unpredictable requirements** in systems development [12].

When dealing with **complexity**, teams experimenting with agile needed to face a number of paradoxes that enabled a range of responses depending on contextual changes. Agile leaders needed to learn how to balance accountability and autonomy, hierarchical control and self-organization, predictability and adaptability, or efficiency and responsiveness. This, alongside with the engineering practices, required a great deal of learning for software development teams.

© Springer Nature Switzerland AG 2019
P. Meirelles et al. (Eds.): WBMA 2019, CCIS 1106, pp. 3–7, 2019.
https://doi.org/10.1007/978-3-030-36701-5_1

Over time, what started being experimented on small teams, for specific situations, finally become mainstream to software development at **scale**. A number of adaptations were developed by industry, shared through community events and investigated by researchers. Examples of this evolution is the Continuous Delivery approach, in which software can be released to production at any time, and the DevOps movement [9].

As concluded by the State of DevOps 2019 report involving over 31,000 professionals (mostly from Global North countries), the industry continues to improve on agility, particularly among the so-called "elite performers". They also conclude, through their research models, that delivering software quickly, reliably, and safely is a core engine of the technology transformation and organizational performance on respondents' organizations [6].

2   Agile Transformations and the Risk of Commodification

Agile ideas scaled not only in size, from teams to the whole organizations, but also in scope. As recently stated by Steve Denning, "we are now seeing Agile in manufacturing, Agile in retail, Agile in petroleum, Agile in strategy, Agile in human resources, Agile budgeting, Agile auditing, and Agile organizational culture" [4]. Agile transformations aiming to achieve organizational (or business) agility are happening in many organizations [13]. The research community is still defining the meaning of agile transformation and the possible research areas to address existent challenges, as how to manage organizational boundaries or how to integrate non-development functions to this new way of organizing work [1].

In the experts' community, there is a debate on how much these ideas are still following the agile principles, if it makes sense to call them "agile" or it is going beyond its essence and meaning. In the same vein, there is a strong debate around failures of agile transformations. One of the main arguments is that many organizations still mimic agile practices, that they do not really grasp (yet) agile principles and values [4]. Often, organizations follow technology trends and behaviors without understanding the cause, but expecting the promoted effects. Because the values and principles need to be well understood to be practiced and finally learned, no matter what specific agile method is in trial, few benefits will be realized.

To address concerns about the risks of agile transformations, there are proposals for frameworks describing principles and, sometimes, recipes for organizations to roll out agile. This is known as the commodification of agile, a tentative to simplify and control the journey, what usually also limits its full realization (because it will be partial or contextual) and can often bring discredit to the movement. Guidance that concentrates on principles are usually more beneficial, because frame the process without being prescriptive. Examples are Bossa Nova [5] and the DevOps Handbook [9].

3   Agility for Broader Positive Impact and Sustainability

Because of the discussions on what is next for agile, in industry or academia, we often refer back to agile roots to remember the fundamental reasons, the essence, why agile in the first place? One of the drivers of agility has been the increased competition at a global scale, where the advantage is transient, and learning and adapting quickly is the way to thrive [10].

So, the fundamental assumption is that agile processes harness change for the customer's competitive advantage. This frequently justifies continuous improvement efforts and investments. It is rare to hear questions on why competitive advantage? Is competitive advantage the final purpose we are all working for? Is competitive advantage sustainable?

For instance, there is already acknowledgment that most successful digital organizations have become (quasi-)monopolies through agility and that sometimes they abuse this power (e.g. on users' privacy). Statements as "business agility is not the same thing as business virtue" [4] are examples of luminaries recognizing the importance of discussions related to positive impact that organizations need to reflect a.

The Agile Manifesto brought a principle related to sustainability, defined as "maintaining a constant pace indefinitely". This principle has been interpreted from managerial, technical, and social aspects. A team should be able to keep its workload under control given the short-term focus. If they do not carry a heavy workload, a traditional problem faced by software development teams, they are less likely to burnout or have work-life balance issues. Finally, from a technical and management perspective, the team should be able to avoid future heavy workloads or stress of not getting anything done by managing technical debit.

In a broader sense, sustainability is meeting the needs of the present without compromising the ability of future generations to meet their needs. It is often considered in terms of the three pillars of environmental, social and economic considerations [8]. The link between sustainability and software development has been done by some research fields, as the nascent *Information and Communication Technologies for Sustainability* (ICT4S)[1].

This research community has created the **Karlskrona Manifesto** [2] to articulate a set of principles and commitments, as we are responsible for the long-term consequences of our systems' designs. They state that "if we don't take sustainability into account when designing, no matter in which domain and for what purpose, we miss the opportunity to cause positive change". A positive impact on society occurs when the effect of a sustainable activity on the social fabric of the community causes well-being of the individuals and families [16].

The Karlskrona Manifesto states that "sustainability is at its heart a systemic concept and has to be understood on a set of dimensions, including social, individual, environmental, economic, and technical". When trying to understand the most important global discussions around sustainability, we usually refer to the 17 universal goals for sustainable economic, social and ecological development to be met by 2030, described as the Sustainable Development Goals (SDGs) [11].

---

[1] http://ict4s.org.

4   Core Agility Capabilities at the Heart of Implementation of SDGs

Implementing sustainable development goals is finding solutions for wicked problems, complex, non-linear, dynamic challenges in situations of insufficient resources, incomplete information, emerging risks and threats, and fast changing environments. Software development, in general, is a complex environment that cannot be fully understood upfront, some experimentation is needed.

In this context, agile principles are appropriate for the exploration of emergent needs, so the agile evolutionary approach is a fit to the experimentation approach that sustainable (wicked) problems require [14]. Agile has brought a huge contribution to the IT community as it created a language, a set of principles, a structure for experimentation and digital innovation through teams. Agile is being successfully connected to other innovation approaches, as Design Thinking and Lean Startups.

The agile movement is now devoted to transform entire organizations, which requires knowledge to redesign them from upside down, breaking silos and re-purposing entire business functions. This required systemic capability is no longer exclusive for solving clients' problems, but to the reinvention of the organizations themselves. This set of sophisticated capabilities can be key levers to promote systemic changes we need for sustainability.

While the assumption that agility enables competitiveness is still valid, how much competitiveness we want to enable and to what price? Is the indefinite evolution of agility towards competitiveness helping society to live more sustainably? Should agility enable cooperativeness among organizations, not only inside them? To answer these questions, professionals need to embrace knowledge on areas as ethics, environment, policy, economics, and social justice. I would argue this is a new purpose for the agile movement, beyond the "compete or die" logic, assuming a more proactive and robust role on sustainability challenges and goals.

Implementing SDGs will require strategic efforts by different actors and transformative actions. There is a need for approaches and principles guiding strategic transformational change for organizations trying to implement SDGs [7]. Therefore, there is an opportunity to investigate how business agility can support the implementation of sustainable development goals. Where are the synergies and incompatibilities and how this knowledge can help society to make a transition to qualitative growth [15].

5   Conclusion

This position paper is a call to action for the agile community to revisit the purpose of agile, re-framing it in the 21st century context. The central argument is built upon the idea that agile evolution is being driven mostly by competitive advantage and scaling forces. From small to large teams, from teams of teams to entire organizations, some of them becoming quasi-monopolies. These drivers not necessarily help society achieving sustainable development goals.

A multi- or trans-disciplinary approach is probably needed to rethink the major drivers of current transformations (for agility and for sustainability) and strategically use the existent agile capabilities.

References

1. Barroca, L., Dingsøyr, T., Mikalsen, M.: Agile transformation: a summary and research agenda from the first international workshop. In: Hoda, R. (ed.) XP 2019. LNBIP, vol. 364, pp. 3–9. Springer, Cham (2019). https://doi.org/10.1007/978-3-030-30126-2_1
2. Becker, C., et al.: The Karlskrona manifesto for sustainability design. CoRR (2014)
3. Commission, E.: The importance of the digital economy. Official website. https://ec.europa.eu/growth/sectors/digital-economy/importance_en
4. Denning, S.: Why agile's future is bright (2019). https://www.forbes.com/sites/stevedenning/2019/08/25/why-the-future-of-agile-is-bright
5. Eckstein, J., Buck, J.: Company-wide Agility with Beyond Budgeting, Open Space & Sociocracy: Survive & Thrive on Disruption: Business Agility with Agile BOSSA nova. CreateSpace Independent Publishing Platform (2018)
6. Forsgren, N., Smith, D., Humble, J., Frazelle, J.: 2019 accelerate state of DevOps report. Technical report (2019). http://cloud.google.com/devops/state-of-devops/
7. Grainger-Brown, J., Malekpour, S.: Implementing the sustainable development goals: a review of strategic tools and frameworks available to organisations. Sustainability 11(5), 1381 (2019). https://www.mdpi.com/2071-1050/11/5/1381
8. Hilty, L.M., Aebischer, B.: ICT for sustainability: an emerging research field. In: Hilty, L.M., Aebischer, B. (eds.) ICT Innovations for Sustainability. AISC, vol. 310, pp. 3–36. Springer, Cham (2015). https://doi.org/10.1007/978-3-319-09228-7_1
9. Kim, G., Humble, J., Debois, P., Willis, J.: The DevOps Handbook: How to Create World-Class Agility, Reliability, and Security in Technology Organizations. IT Revolution Press, ITpro collection (2016)
10. McGrath, R., Gourlay, A.: The End of Competitive Advantage: How to Keep Your Strategy Moving as Fast as Your Business. Harvard Business Review Press, Brighton (2013)
11. Nations, U.: Multi-stakeholder forum on science, technology and innovation for the sustainable development goals: summary by the co-chairs. Technical report, United Nations, June 2016
12. de Melo, C.O., et al.: The evolution of agile software development in Brazil - education, research, and the state-of-the-practice. J. Braz. Comput. Soc. 19(4), 523–552 (2013)
13. Olszewska, M., Heidenberg, J., Weijola, M., Mikkonen, K., Porres, I.: Quantitatively measuring a large-scale agile transformation. J. Syst. Softw. 117, 258–273 (2016)
14. Pelrine, J.: On understanding software agility - a social complexity point of view. Emergence Complex. Organ. 13, 26–37 (2011)
15. Renn, O., Goble, R., Kastenholz, H.: How to apply the concept of sustainability to a region. Technol. Forecast. Soc. Change 58(1), 63–81 (1998)
16. de Sousa, T.C., Melo, C.O.: Sustainable infrastructure, industrial ecology and eco-innovation: positive impact on society. In: Leal Filho, W., Azul, A., Brandli, L., Özuyar, P., Wall, T. (eds) Industry, Innovation and Infrastructure. Encyclopedia of the UN Sustainable Development Goals, pp. 1–10. Springer, Cham (2019). https://doi.org/10.1007/978-3-319-71059-4

Empirical Studies on Agile

An Empirical Study of Test-Driven Development vs. Test-Last Development Using Eye Tracking

Joelma Choma[1]([✉]), Eduardo M. Guerra[1], Tiago Silva da Silva[2],
Thomas Albuquerque[2], Vanessa G. Albuquerque[3], and Luciana M. Zaina[4]

[1] National Institute for Space Research, São José dos Campos, Brazil
jh.choma@hotmail.com, guerraem@gmail.com
[2] Federal University of São Paulo, São José dos Campos, Brazil
silvadasilva@gmail.com, tealbthomas@gmail.com
[3] Group Being Educational, Guarulhos, Brazil
vanessa.ga@gmail.com
[4] Federal University of São Carlos, Sorocaba, Brazil
lzaina@ufscar.br

Abstract. Test-Driven Development (TDD) is an iterative software development technique in which unit tests are defined before production code, while Test-Last Development (TLD) is a more traditional development technique in which unit tests are written after the features are implemented. There have been a number of empirical studies investigating the effects of TDD compared to other approaches in terms of software quality and productivity. However, there are few investigations in which the TDD effects are explored from the viewpoint of the developers' experience. This paper presents an eye-tracking study carried out in order to measure visual attention during the coding and test tasks when developers are using TDD compared to TLD. Our preliminary findings pointed out a similar visual effort proportion in both techniques, but a difference regarding eye gaze behavior between them which needs to be confirmed.

Keywords: Test-Driven Development · TDD · Test-Last Development · TLD · Eye tracking

1 Introduction

Test-Driven Development (TDD) [3] is a technique for designing and developing software that is widely adopted by agile software development teams. TDD was proposed by Kent Beck in the late 1990s as a key practice of the Extreme Programming (XP). Popularized by XP, TDD has been considered a standalone process nowadays [26]. The single most important rule in TDD is writing test cases for what is about to code. This dynamic is referred to as "Test-First" in which the tests are used for specification purposes in addition to verification

© Springer Nature Switzerland AG 2019
P. Meirelles et al. (Eds.): WBMA 2019, CCIS 1106, pp. 11–24, 2019.
https://doi.org/10.1007/978-3-030-36701-5_2

and validation. By following this practice to writing unit tests before coding, the software can be incrementally developed without a need for detailed designing it upfront, since developers are engaged to think ahead of the functionality [17]. In Test-Last Development (TLD), tests are traditionally built after the features are implemented only for verification and validation purposes [31].

Over the last decade, several empirical studies have investigated the effects of TDD compared to TLD from the perspective of developer productivity and software quality (internal and external) [14,22,37]. However, few empirical studies have explored the TDD effects from the viewpoint of the developers' experience [31,32]. Software development is an intellectual activity that encompasses affective, cognitive, conative, and social aspects, going far beyond mere technical aspects [25]. Tools, techniques, methods, and development processes can be best understood to be designed or improved when studies can capture the involvement of the developers with different aspects related to the development processes, modeling methods, and other tasks [12].

In this paper, we present an eye-tracking study on developers' experience in applying TDD and TLD. This study was performed in a user experience lab involving eight developers with different experience levels and skills. An eye tracker (hardware and software) was used to monitor the developer's visual attention via eye-movements data during implementation and test tasks using TDD and TLD. We addressed two research question in this study:

- RQ1: How is visual attention distributed over implementation and test tasks when developers are using TDD compared to TLD?
- RQ2: What are the differences in eye gaze behavior between TDD and TLD presented in this study?

To answer RQ1, we choose visual effort metrics to analyze the developers' visual attention based on the two eye gaze data: (i) number of fixations and (ii) duration of fixations. Fixations refer to a focused state when the eye remains still over a while. It is a voluntary movement that can last from 200–300 ms to up to several seconds. The number of fixations indicates the number of times that a user looked to a certain area of interest (AoI), and the fixation duration indicates the period that a user looked to a certain AoI. To answer RQ2, we conducted a qualitative analysis using gaze plots. A gaze plot displays a static view of the eye gaze data for each area of interest, allowing to visualize the length of the fixation and sequence of fixations (scan paths).

This paper is structured as follows: Sect. 2 provides related work. Section 3 describes the eye-tracking study design. Section 4 presents the study results and their analysis. Section 5 presents the discussion, conclusions and future work.

2   Related Work

2.1   Test-Driven Development

TDD process embraces a set of successive short cycles to develop the desired functionality by following three steps: (1) write a test for the next bit of functionality you want to add; (2) write the functional code until the test passes; and

(3) refactor both new and old code to make it well-structured [3]. The refactoring activity is strongly recommended in both TDD and TLD to change the production and test code and make it as simple as possible, ensuring that all tests pass [18]. Tests frameworks such as JUnit [4] were developed to enable and facilitate the implementation of unit tests. Creating unit tests is important because they help to ensure the system works correctly, mostly after code refactoring [10].

Most of the reported evidence on TDD refers to aspects of productivity (e.g., the overall time required to develop a feature), internal code quality (e.g., number of defects), and external code quality (e.g., complexity, code coverage, coupling, and cohesion between objects) [36,37]. There are a number of controlled experiments that have been done based on objective measurements [11,14,22]. However, there are still few studies in which the effects of TDD are explored from the perceptions of developers [8,32].

Gupta and Jalote [17] evaluated the impact of TDD on activities like designing, coding, and testing. Their results suggest that TDD can be more efficient regarding development efforts and the developer's productivity. Vu et al. [38] examined the TDD effects regarding software quality, and their results indicated that TDD did not outperform TLD in many quality measures. In a survey with practitioners about efficiency and quality of test cases, George and Williams [15] found that, for most of them, the TDD practice helps to create designs that are less complicated and easier to understand.

Janzen and Saiedian [20] revealed in their study that mature developers are much more likely to adopt TDD than early programmers. Scanniello et al. [32] reported that novices tend to believe more than professionals that TDD improves productivity. Munir et al. [26] by conducting a controlled experiment with professional Java developers found that the majority of participants favor TLD over TDD due to factors such as lower level of the learning curve and a minimum effort needed to maintain and understand TLD compared to TDD.

Until now, there is no consensus on results comparing the two approaches since each experience involves different contexts and potential influence factors [20]. For example, Shull et al. [36] concluded that moderate evidence exists to claim that TDD tends to improve the code's external quality, while evidence about productivity was inconclusive. For some researchers, TDD can decrease productivity because the majority of the time is devoted to the creation of tests instead of production code [24]. Some approaches involving automatic recognition systems have been proposed for conformance assessment and understanding the development behavior underlying TDD [5]. Within this context, we believe that understanding the dynamics of TDD and TLD from the developer's experience can provide important insights to researchers and practitioners, for example, improve tools or methods for training people or for supporting the development process.

2.2 Eye-Tracking in Software Engineering

In software engineering (SE), the eye-tracking technology was introduced in the early nineties by Crosby and Stelovsky [9] to explore the way developers were reading an algorithm written in Pascal. Ever since then, eye-trackers have evolved in terms of effectiveness and usability. This technology has been used mainly in human-computer interaction research [19]. Its use within research in software engineering has been restricted because of the high cost of the devices which still not easy to be gained by many researchers [27].

Sharafi et al. [34] described a set of experiments that used eye-trackers in software engineering research. More recently, Obaidellah et al. [27] also provided a mapping of the studies reporting how the experiments used eye-trackers, including information regarding experimental setup, subjects, artifacts, tasks, metrics, and type of trackers. According to these secondary studies, most engineering software researchers have used eye tracking in tasks related to model comprehension such as UML diagrams [21,29,35], code comprehension [6,7,30], and debugging [1,13,16].

In the agile context, Pietinen et al. [28] have investigated the interplay between pair-programming productivity and recorded developers' eye movements. In this work, they described some problems and limitations when eye tracking is used to study pair programming. In general, few eye-tracking studies consider the interaction of users with external resources, those are outside the areas of interests delimited on the computer screen.

To date, there are few studies using eye-tracking to explore more complex tasks related to development practices and processes. Moreover, most of the experiments involve simple tasks to be performed in a short time (10 to 30 min), and studies exploring longer processes tend to be scarce. As far as we know, no previous study has used eye-tracking to explore dynamic aspects of TDD.

3   Study Design

Following the Goal-Question-Metric (GQM) approach [2], the main goal of the study was to *analyze* the software development using TDD and TLD *for the purpose of* evaluating dynamic aspects *with respect to* the visual attention required for implementation and test from the point of view of the researcher *in the context of* user experience laboratory.

3.1   Subjects

The study participants were eight software developers from the postgraduate program at the Brazilian National Institute for Space Research (INPE). They were Master's degree students from different experience levels. As presented in Table 1, we collected the following demographic data for each participant: years of experience in programming, years of experience in Java language, level of experience in TDD. Based on this information, we divided the participants into two groups (TDD and TLD) to have two balanced groups in terms of programming experience and background.

All subjects were male and had normal vision. Only one of them wore corrective lenses. Before the study, the subjects signed an informed consent form that provided an overview of the experimental procedures. However, they were not aware of the research questions.

Table 1. Participants' experience

Group	Subject	Programming	Java	TDD
TDD	S1	3–5 years	3–5 years	Beginner
	S2	Over 10 years	6–10 years	Beginner
	S3	3–5 years	3–5 years	Beginner
	S4	Over 10 years	Over 10 years	Intermediate
TLD	S5	Over 10 years	1–2 years	Beginner
	S6	3–5 years	1–2 years	Beginner
	S7	Over 10 years	Over 10 years	Beginner
	S8	Over 10 years	6–10 years	Intermediate

3.2 Study Setting

The study was conducted in a user experience laboratory using the Tobii T60 eye-tracker[1] to capture different data related to eye movements and eye gaze. Through an unobtrusive data collection, the equipment provides eye gaze data which include timestamps, gaze positions, eye positions, pupil size, and validity codes. In this study, we used gaze positions and timestamps to measure visual effort. The equipment was attached and configured on a 25-in. screen (PC-1). This first screen was used by the study subjects to perform the method implementation and testing tasks, where we previously prepared the development environment. A Java code project using JUnit as a testing framework was created on the Eclipse IDE[2]. The screen was split into three areas which displayed the execution window of the unit tests, the method implementation, and the test code, placed one next to the other. On a table on the right side, we provide a 15-in. laptop (PC-2) to access the specification document and web page for searching, displayed in overlapping pages. During the study sessions, the interactions of the participants could be observed through a glass wall by the researcher who played the role of moderator.

3.3 Tasks

The task of the participants was to create in the Java language a method to transform a camelCase string into a list of strings with common words. That is, given a word as input it must be necessarily a camelCase string instance, and the output must be a list of instances of common words. Based on the pilot test,

---

[1] https://www.tobiipro.com.
[2] https://www.eclipse.org.

we defined four test cases. Table 2 presents the four input and output examples that participants should implement and use as a basis for their testing. We selected four participants to implement this task using TDD, while the remaining participants would implement it using TLD.

Table 2. Input and output for camelCase conversion method

Test case#	Inputs in camelCase	Outputs in string list
1	name	"name"
2	Name	"name"
3	compoundName	"name", "compound"
4	recover10First	"recover", "10", "first"

3.4   Areas of Interest (AoI)

Eye movements focus a person's visual attention to the parts of a visual stimulus when trying to understand and solve a given task [23]. In this study, the eye tracker was used to recorded eye movements and detect where the subject was looking at on the screen during the implementation and test tasks – the two visual stimuli. As shown in Fig. 1, we defined two areas of interest: (AoI-1) area of implementation where the developer implements the method and (AoI-2) area of testing where the developer writes the unit tests.

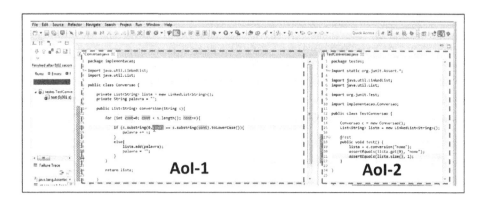

Fig. 1. Areas of interest defined on the Java project

3.5   Variables

A wide variety of eye-tracking metrics has been utilized to measure the visual effort in different types of SE tasks. Sharafi et al. [33] categorized such metrics in four groups: (1) metrics based on fixations, (2) metrics based on saccades,

(3) metrics based on scanpaths, and (4) metrics of pupil size and blink rate. However, the most common types of eye-tracking metrics are based on the number of fixations and the duration of fixation. The number of fixations indicates the number of times that a user looked to a certain area of interest (AoI), while the fixation duration indicates the period that a user looked to a certain AoI [34].

In this study, we were using six variables to cover the two areas of interest (implementation and test), which use the main two main types of eye gaze data: fixation count, the average fixation duration, and total fixation duration.

The variables are described as follows:

- Fixation Count on Implementation FC(I): The total number of eye fixations on the area of interest concerning the implementation of the camelCase conversion method. This refers to the entire method implementation.
- Fixation Count on Testing FC(T): The total number of eye fixations on the area of interest concerning unit test writing. This refers to the entire tests writing.
- Average Fixation Duration on Implementation AFD(I): The average length of time of all fixations in the area of interest concerning the implementation of the camelCase conversion method.
- Average Fixation Duration on Test AFD(T): The average length of time of all fixations in the area of interest concerning unit test writing.
- Total Fixation Duration on Implementation TFD(I): The total length of time of all fixations in the area of interest concerning the implementation of the camelCase conversion method.
- Total Fixation Duration on Test TFD(T): The total length of time of all fixations in the area of interest concerning unit test writing.

The first two measures are based on eye fixations, where a higher fixation count indicates more effort needed by subjects to solve the task. The last four measures are based on eye fixation duration, where the more time spent implementing the method or writing the tests indicates more effort needed by subjects to solve the task. The unit of measure is seconds.

3.6 Procedure

At the beginning of each section, the moderator performed the eye-tracker calibration for each participant. During the calibration, five points are displayed on the screen and mapped their locations with the coordinates of the participants' eye movements. With some participants, the calibration was repeated one more time with of purpose to achieve the highest possible accuracy.

After calibration of the equipment, the next screen displayed instructions on the task. The moderator guided the participants regarding the task to be performed in PC-1 and showed the requirements document and the web page for searching located in the PC-2. The moderator clarified to the participants that only general doubts about java syntax were allowed to be searched from the internet. Also, it was established that, participants could only use basic Java language API classes for method development. Therefore, the use of external components was not allowed.

Finally, the participants were told that they would have approximately one hour to complete their tasks. After development activity, we had them fill out a post-test questionnaire, with the objective of gathering their perceptions about the technique used in the development (TDD or TLD) and the difficulties they encountered during the execution of the task.

4   Results

The results of the study in terms of developers' performance showed that only three participants were able to complete the task successfully developing all test cases, with one performed the tasks in 22 min (S3), while the other two took just over an hour (S4 and S8). In the TDD group, the participant S1 did not perform the last two test cases, and the participant S2, who had a great potential to complete the entire task, forgot to implement the test case 2 or did not do it for some reason still unknown. In the TLD group, the participant S6 was unable to conclude the last test case. Unfortunately, two participants who had used TLD (S5 and S7) were unable to complete any test cases.

Table 3 shows the time spent in minutes and the proportional time (%) spent on each test cases (TC) performed by each participant. Proportional time for each test case (see Table 2) was computed as a ratio of time spent on a test case to the overall time spent on the task. By analyzing the proportion of dedicated time, we intended to identify which test cases were easier or more difficult to solve. However, the results indicated that the participants of the two groups had different degrees of difficulty.

Table 3. Time spent in minutes and the proportional time (%)

Group	Subject	Time spent	TC1	TC2	TC3	TC4
TDD	S1	75	0.61	0.39	–	–
	S2	57	0.30	–	0.59	0.11
	S3	22	0.35	0.11	0.50	0.04
	S4	64	0.08	0.02	0.41	0.49
TLD	S5	75	1.00	–	–	–
	S6	76	0.21	0.09	0.22	0.48
	S7	74	1.00	–	–	–
	S8	67	0.55	0.04	0.03	0.38

4.1   Visual Attention Analysis (RQ1)

To verify how developers' visual attention was distributed over implementation and test tasks (RQ1), we analyzed the visual effort metrics related to the number of fixations (FC) and the duration of fixation (AFD and TFD). Table 4 presents the results, where the values in brackets (next to the fixation count values) refer to the proportion of fixations in each area of interest concerning the total fixations individually captured. The proportional fixation count for each area was computed as a ratio of fixation count on an area to the overall fixation time on two areas. On average, in terms of fixation count, participants in both groups had approximately 76.2% visual effort on the area of implementation and 23.8% visual effort on the test area.

As for AFD(I), we found lower fixation gaze time by participant S3 the one who solved the task faster using TDD. Participant S8 using TLD had the longest fixation time in the implementation area. Concerning AFD(T), two participants using TDD (S1 and S3) and two participants using TLD (S5 and S6) had a longer fixation time in the test area than implementation area. However, concerning total fixations duration (TFD), all participants in the two groups had a longer total fixation gaze duration in the area of implementation. The visual effort of the participant S6 using TLD was almost twice as high as the other participants, both in the implementation and in the test.

When analyzing the TFD(I) results of the two subjects who successfully completed the task almost within the same time (S4 and S8), we found both developers had a similar total fixation gaze duration in the area of implementation. However, the total fixation duration in the test area of the participant who used TDD (S4) was significantly lower than the participant who used TLD (S8).

Table 4. Number of fixations and the duration of fixation metrics

Group	Subject	FC(I)	FC(T)	AFD(I)	AFD(T)	TFD(I)	TFD(T)
TDD	S1	2414 (59.6%)	1636 (40.4%)	0.23	0.33	584.16	359.19
	S2	2667 (71.6%)	1058 (28.4%)	0.13	0.04	668.66	169.71
	S3	1177 (64.1%)	659 (35.9%)	0.05	0.07	251.2	122.45
	S4	3632 (96.4%)	137 (3.6%)	0.22	0.17	899.67	29.03
TLD	S5	1143 (86.9%)	173 (13.1%)	0.1	0.15	135.8	19.9
	S6	5492 (77.3%)	1613 (22.7%)	0.09	0.17	1680.5	488.57
	S7	3324 (77.0%)	993 (23.0%)	0.17	0.17	779.02	221.66
	S8	4329 (81.4%)	988 (18.6%)	0.25	0.14	982.41	241.07

FC-Fixation Count|AFD-Average Fixation Duration|TFD-Total Fixation Duration
I - Implementation of the method | T - Test code

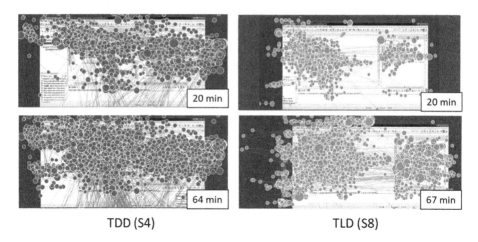

TDD (S4)   TLD (S8)

Fig. 2. Static view of the eye gaze for implementation and test from TDD and TLD.

4.2 Qualitative Analysis (RQ2)

To verify differences in eye gaze behavior by comparing TDD and TLD (RQ2), we only analyzed the gaze plots of the two subjects who completed the task successfully in similar timing (S3 and S4), respectively using TDD and TLD. Figure 2 shows two gaze plots for each developer. The first two gaze plots display the static views after 20 min of developing, and the last two plots display the static views in the final time of completion of tasks. As shown in the gaze plots, the circles represent the fixation dots, which the radius is proportional with the fixation duration, while the lines represent the eye movements (saccades) which connect fixation dots.

When comparing TDD and TLD plots, we found two different behavior. The interaction between both implementation and test tasks seems to be more intense in TDD than TLD. That is, the fixation dots cover the two AoIs more uniformly in the gaze plots of TDD. While, in the TLD, the gaze plots showed a larger space not filled between the two AoIs, which to allow us to notice that implementation and tests were worked in separate times.

5   Discussion and Conclusion

The study was designed to be completed in less than 60 min to avoid the fatigue effect [30]. With more time, maybe more subjects could have been able to complete their tasks. We sought to balance the distribution of the subjects based on their experience levels. However, when analyzing the performance of participants, we noticed that each subject had its own pace of development and different skills for problem-solving. We observed that different experience levels, preferences, and reasoning processes could impact on rhythms and patterns of development, as pointed out by Wang and Erdogmus [39]. Furthermore, programmers tend to define the best way to work in a given context.

We analyzed the subjects' behaviors individually by using descriptive statistics rather than inferential one because the sample was small. We recognized that the low number of participants did not favor ensuring well-balanced groups, since in the TLD group, for instance, only one developer was able to solve the task successfully. To mitigate this threat, we could increase the statistical power of the study. However, finding experienced TDD practitioners who are available to participate in this kind of research is a challenge [5].

As for the distribution of visual attention (RQ1), the fixation count results suggest that, on average, the implementation and testing effort have similar proportion in both development techniques (TDD and TLD). At first glance, the average duration of the fixations seems to be directly related to the subjects' skills. The subject with the best performance (S3) had a low fixation gaze time in the two areas of interest. However, something that caught our attention was the fact that this particular participant had declared experience of fewer than 5 years (both programming and Java) and to be a beginner in TDD. In the post-test questionnaire, this participant stated had no problem with implementing TDD. He further stated that TDD helped him in the implementation of the proposed tasks since he was induced to implement it in parts, completing the tasks without drawbacks.

Another participant who completed the task using TDD (S4) is a more experienced programmer and with an intermediate knowledge in TDD. However, his fixation gaze time was higher than the fixation gaze time of the S3. In the post-test questionnaire, he also stated no problem during the tasks. Within the same group, by comparing the two subjects (S3 and S4), we noticed that the participant with more experience in TDD had a low number of fixations and also a smaller total fixation duration in the area of the test (AoI2). Analyzing the individual behavior, we could see that S4 had a greater effort in writing the tests at the beginning of the development. However, this effort was softened over time, and then his focus turned to the implementation of the method. Nevertheless, further investigations will be needed to verify if this fact is related to the experience background with TDD.

About the difference in eye gaze behavior between TDD and TLD (RQ2), we found differences by observing static views of two of the participants. However, such behavior needs to be verified in future work by considering a larger sampling. If such behavior is confirmed as a pattern between the two techniques, we can try to investigate the impact of each technique from the point of view of cognitive effort, for example.

Overall, existing studies when comparing TDD and TLD focus their analyses on the final results of the code and whether the tests were written first or not. In contrast to this, we are interested in understanding the dynamics of the development process underlying the two techniques. Thus, we focused on the dynamic part of the development process and the developers' activity during the tasks. The main contribution of this study is to characterize the TDD and TLD techniques from the developers' experience. This paper presents our preliminary results in this direction.

In future work, more studies are needed to confirm the findings on development patterns meet when we analyzed the eye gaze data using gaze plots. Further, we intend to analyze the developers' visual attention considering the external resources available in the study environment such as the requirements specification document and searching sources.

Acknowledgment. This study was financed in part by the Coordenação de Aperfeiçoamento de Pessoal de Nível Superior - Brasil (CAPES) - Finance Code 001. Also, we would like to thank the support granted by Brazilian funding agency FAPESP (grant 2014/16236-6 and 2014/25779-3, São Paulo Research Foundation).

References

1. Barik, T., et al.: Do developers read compiler error messages? In: Proceedings of the 39th International Conference on Software Engineering, pp. 575–585. IEEE Press (2017)
2. Basili, V.R., Caldiera, G., Rombach, H.D.: The goal question metric approach. Encyclopedia of Software Engineering, pp. 528–532 (1994)
3. Beck, K.: Test-Driven Development: By Example. Addison-Wesley Professional, Boston (2002)
4. Beck, K.: JUnit Pocket Guide: Quick Look-up and Advice. O'Reilly Media Inc., Sebastopol (2004)
5. Becker, K., Pedroso, B.D.S.C., Pimenta, M.S., Jacobi, R.P.: Besouro: a framework for exploring compliance rules in automatic TDD behavior assessment. Inf. Softw. Technol. **57**, 494–508 (2015)
6. Bednarik, R., Tukiainen, M.: Analysing and interpreting quantitative eye-tracking data in studies of programming: phases of debugging with multiple representations. In: Proceedings of the 19th Annual Workshop of the Psychology of Programming Interest Group (PPIG 2007), Joensuu, Finland, pp. 158–172. Citeseer (2007)
7. Busjahn, T., et al.: Eye movements in code reading: relaxing the linear order. In: Proceedings of the 23rd International Conference on Program Comprehension, pp. 255–265. IEEE (2015)
8. Choma, J., Guerra, E.M., da Silva, T.S.: Developers' initial perceptions on TDD practice: a thematic analysis with distinct domains and languages. In: Garbajosa, J., Wang, X., Aguiar, A. (eds.) XP 2018. LNBIP, vol. 314, pp. 68–85. Springer, Cham (2018). https://doi.org/10.1007/978-3-319-91602-6_5
9. Crosby, M.E., Stelovsky, J.: How do we read algorithms? A case study. Computer **23**(1), 25–35 (1990)
10. Deng, C., Wilson, P., Maurer, F.: FitClipse: a fit-based eclipse plug-in for executable acceptance test driven development. In: Concas, G., Damiani, E., Scotto, M., Succi, G. (eds.) XP 2007. LNCS, vol. 4536, pp. 93–100. Springer, Heidelberg (2007). https://doi.org/10.1007/978-3-540-73101-6_13
11. Desai, C., Janzen, D., Savage, K.: A survey of evidence for test-driven development in academia. ACM SIGCSE Bull. **40**(2), 97–101 (2008)
12. Fagerholm, F., Münch, J.: Developer experience: concept and definition. In: Proceedings of the International Conference on Software and System Process, pp. 73–77. IEEE Press (2012)

13. Fritz, T., Begel, A., Müller, S.C., Yigit-Elliott, S., Züger, M.: Using psycho-physiological measures to assess task difficulty in software development. In: Proceedings of the 36th International Conference on Software Engineering, pp. 402–413. ACM (2014)

14. Fucci, D., et al.: An external replication on the effects of test-driven development using a multi-site blind analysis approach. In: Proceedings of the 10th ACM/IEEE International Symposium on Empirical Software Engineering and Measurement, p. 3. ACM (2016)

15. George, B., Williams, L.: A structured experiment of test-driven development. Inf. Softw. Technol. **46**(5), 337–342 (2004)

16. Goswami, A., Walia, G., McCourt, M., Padmanabhan, G.: Using eye tracking to investigate reading patterns and learning styles of software requirement inspectors to enhance inspection team outcome. In: Proceedings of the 10th ACM/IEEE International Symposium on Empirical Software Engineering and Measurement, p. 34. ACM (2016)

17. Gupta, A., Jalote, P.: An experimental evaluation of the effectiveness and efficiency of the test driven development. In: Proceedings of the First International Symposium on Empirical Software Engineering and Measurement, pp. 285–294. IEEE Computer Society (2007)

18. Ivo, A.A.S., Guerra, E.M.: ReTest: framework for applying TDD in the development of non-deterministic algorithms. In: Silva da Silva, T., Estácio, B., Kroll, J., Mantovani Fontana, R. (eds.) WBMA 2016. CCIS, vol. 680, pp. 72–84. Springer, Cham (2017). https://doi.org/10.1007/978-3-319-55907-0_7

19. Jacob, R.J., Karn, K.S.: Eye tracking in human-computer interaction and usability research: ready to deliver the promises. In: The Mind's Eye, pp. 573–605. Elsevier (2003)

20. Janzen, D.S., Saiedian, H.: A leveled examination of test-driven development acceptance. In: Proceedings of the 29th International Conference on Software Engineering (ICSE 2007), pp. 719–722. IEEE (2007)

21. Jeanmart, S., Gueheneuc, Y.G., Sahraoui, H., Habra, N.: Impact of the visitor pattern on program comprehension and maintenance. In: Proceedings of the 3rd International Symposium on Empirical Software Engineering and Measurement, pp. 69–78. IEEE Computer Society (2009)

22. Jeffries, R., Melnik, G.: Guest editors' introduction: TDD-the art of fearless programming. IEEE Softw. **24**(3), 24–30 (2007)

23. Kanwisher, N., Wojciulik, E.: Visual attention: insights from brain imaging. Nat. Rev. Neurosci. **1**(2), 91 (2000)

24. Khanam, Z., Ahsan, M.N.: Evaluating the effectiveness of test driven development: advantages and pitfalls. Int. J. Appl. Eng. Res. **12**(18), 7705–7716 (2017)

25. Kuusinen, K., Petrie, H., Fagerholm, F., Mikkonen, T.: Flow, intrinsic motivation, and developer experience in software engineering. In: Sharp, H., Hall, T. (eds.) XP 2016. LNBIP, vol. 251, pp. 104–117. Springer, Cham (2016). https://doi.org/10.1007/978-3-319-33515-5_9

26. Munir, H., Wnuk, K., Petersen, K., Moayyed, M.: An experimental evaluation of test driven development vs. test-last development with industry professionals. In: Proceedings of the 18th International Conference on Evaluation and Assessment in Software Engineering, p. 50. ACM (2014)

27. Obaidellah, U., Al Haek, M., Cheng, P.C.H.: A survey on the usage of eye-tracking in computer programming. ACM Comput. Surv. (CSUR) **51**(1), 5 (2018)

28. Pietinen, S., Bednarik, R., Tukiainen, M.: Shared visual attention in collaborative programming: a descriptive analysis. In: Proceedings of the Workshop on Cooperative and Human Aspects of Software Engineering, pp. 21–24. ACM (2010)
29. Porras, G.C., Guéhéneuc, Y.G.: An empirical study on the efficiency of different design pattern representations in UML class diagrams. Empirical Softw. Eng. **15**(5), 493–522 (2010)
30. Rodeghero, P., McMillan, C., McBurney, P.W., Bosch, N., D'Mello, S.: Improving automated source code summarization via an eye-tracking study of programmers. In: Proceedings of the 36th International Conference on Software Engineering, pp. 390–401. ACM (2014)
31. Romano, S., Fucci, D., Scanniello, G., Turhan, B., Juristo, N.: Results from an ethnographically-informed study in the context of test driven development. In: Proceedings of the 20th International Conference on Evaluation and Assessment in Software Engineering, p. 10. ACM (2016)
32. Scanniello, G., Romano, S., Fucci, D., Turhan, B., Juristo, N.: Students' and professionals' perceptions of test-driven development: a focus group study. In: Proceedings of the 31st Annual ACM Symposium on Applied Computing, pp. 1422–1427. ACM (2016)
33. Sharafi, Z., Shaffer, T., Sharif, B., Guéhéneuc, Y.G.: Eye-tracking metrics in software engineering. In: 2015 Asia-Pacific Software Engineering Conference (APSEC), pp. 96–103. IEEE (2015)
34. Sharafi, Z., Soh, Z., Guéhéneuc, Y.G.: A systematic literature review on the usage of eye-tracking in software engineering. Inf. Softw. Technol. **67**, 79–107 (2015)
35. Sharif, B., Maletic, J.I.: An eye tracking study on the effects of layout in understanding the role of design patterns. In: 2010 IEEE International Conference on Software Maintenance (ICSM), pp. 1–10. IEEE (2010)
36. Shull, F., Melnik, G., Turhan, B., Layman, L., Diep, M., Erdogmus, H.: What do we know about test-driven development? IEEE Softw. **27**(6), 16–19 (2010)
37. Turhan, B., Layman, L., Diep, M., Erdogmus, H., Shull, F.: How effective is test-driven development. In: Making Software: What Really Works, and Why We Believe It, pp. 207–217 (2010)
38. Vu, J.H., Frojd, N., Shenkel-Therolf, C., Janzen, D.S.: Evaluating test-driven development in an industry-sponsored capstone project. In: Proceedings of the Sixth International Conference on Information Technology: New Generations, pp. 229–234. IEEE (2009)
39. Wang, Y., Erdogmus, H.: The role of process measurement in test-driven development. In: Zannier, C., Erdogmus, H., Lindstrom, L. (eds.) XP/Agile Universe 2004. LNCS, vol. 3134, pp. 32–42. Springer, Heidelberg (2004). https://doi.org/10.1007/978-3-540-27777-4_4

On the Mapping of Underlying Concepts of a Combined Use of Lean and User-Centered Design with Agile Development: The Case Study of the Transformation Process of an IT Company

Cassiano Moralles[1]([✉]) [ID], Matheus Vaccaro[1] [ID], Maximilian Zorzetti[1] [ID],
Eliana Pereira[2], Cássio Trindade[1], Bruna Prauchner[1], Sabrina Marczak[1],
and Ricardo Bastos[1]

[1] MunDDoS Research Group – PPGCC – School of Technology, Pontifícia
Universidade Católica do Rio Grande do Sul (PUCRS), Porto Alegre, RS, Brazil
{cassiano.mora,matheus.vaccaro,maximilian.zorzetti,
bruna.prauchner}@acad.pucrs.br,
{cassio.trindade,sabrina.marczak,bastos}@pucrs.br
[2] Instituto Federal do Rio Grande do Sul (IFRS), Porto Alegre, RS, Brazil
eliana.pereira@restinga.ifrs.edu.br

Abstract. The agile development of software requires new approaches
to serve users and end customers. The combination of Lean and User-
Centered Design with Agile gives software development a competitive
advantage. Given the novelty and scarcity of studies on such combined
use in software development, as part of our long-term research that aims
to develop a maturity model to accelerate the transformation from agile
to the use of the combined approaches, we posed as our first step to identify what are the underlying concepts involved on the use of agile, lean,
and user-centered design. We first conducted multiple literature reviews
to identify the concepts for each of the individual approaches to then
conduct an empirical study in order to identify what is considered useful
by two software teams of a multinational IT company that are going
through such a transformation for about 6 months. Our study revealed
that there are concepts from literature not yet considered in practice and
the other way around, there are practiced concepts not found in literature. For now, we hypothesize that this is due to the early maturing
process of the studied teams. We believe that this is an initial contribution that can be of help for other teams enduring this challenging
transformation process. Our research will next investigate how the three
approaches relate to one another in order to provide a unique and con-
solidated combined model of concepts that will further be used as the
skeleton of our maturity model.

Keywords: Agile development · Lean · User-Centered Design ·
Organizational transformation · Empirical study

© Springer Nature Switzerland AG 2019
P. Meirelles et al. (Eds.): WBMA 2019, CCIS 1106, pp. 25–40, 2019.
https://doi.org/10.1007/978-3-030-36701-5_3

1 Introduction

The adoption of agile methodologies has become an industry standard in the past years. Although these methodologies prepare teams to be more adaptive and to keep a closer contact with clients and customers, some authors (e.g., [19]) argue that agile needs to be combined with other approaches in order to provide better guidance for agile teams to improve their understanding of the problem at hand so as to provide more aligned solutions and to keep the customer engaged. To that end, Pivotal Software, Inc.[1] (henceforth referred to as Pivotal) has developed a three-pronged approach to software development: Pivotal Labs.

Pivotal Labs [8] combines certain aspects of Extreme Programming (XP) [1,2], Lean [12,13], and User-Centered Design (UCD) [4,11,15]. Ideas and practices from each of these methodologies are used to tackle different aspects of software development: XP handles the technical activities; Lean mitigates the risk of building the wrong software; and UCD guarantees the software solves an end-user real problem. Software development teams that have adopted this approach show increased productivity and efficacy [16,17], while in our study experience also reporting increased levels of satisfaction and happiness at work.

Apart from the argumentation for the combined use of the approaches from literature (e.g., [19]) and the reports from Pivotal customers, little is known on how to proceed to use XP, Lean, and UCD together. There are, however, comparable studies presenting frameworks that integrate Agile, Lean Startup, and Design Thinking. Grossman-Kahn and Rosensweig present Nordstrom's Innovation Labs model for innovation, *Discovery by Design* [7], while sharing lessons learned from building an innovation capability from the ground up. With a great focus on the needs of the customers and an iterative mindset, they perform rapid experimentation, prototyping, and testing cycles based on the core mindsets and tools from those three methodologies to create innovative products. Dobrigkeit, de Paula, and Uflacker present a software development process called InnoDev [5] based specifically on Scrum, Lean Startup, and Design Thinking. Its process is divided into three phases: Design Thinking, Initial Development, and Development; each composed of a list of activities, roles, deliverables, and techniques. Still, to the best of our knowledge, there are no papers on how a software team should start the journey of a combined adoption of XP, Lean, and UCD, and on how to identify that the team is maturing.

To fill in this gap, we have set up a three-years long research project to investigate the matter. Our main goal is to, at the end of this period, define a maturity model to help software teams through this transformation. Secondarily, we aim to define an assessment method (or, a health check) for identifying the maturity the team presents at a certain moment in time. To do so, our first step is to identify what are the underlying concepts that represent the combined

---

[1] https://pivotal.io.

use of XP, Lean, and UCD. For that, we conducted a series of literature review studies[2] to identify the concepts from literature and from Pivotal Labs[3].

Given this context, in this paper we present a case study of two software development teams from a multinational IT company named ORG (name omitted for confidential reasons). Due to a recent drive to modernize the company from the inside out, these two teams have recently adopted Pivotal Labs, having learned the approach from Pivotal itself. As part of the partnership between our research group and ORG, we have them stationed in a local modern software development lab within the University campus where teams from ORG spend 3 months working in this isolated environment that was intentionally designed to serve our research purposes and to allow the teams to work without interference from others that have not on-boarded the transformation process yet. The main goal of this report is *to present the mapping between literature and practice regarding the underlying concepts that relate to XP, Lean, and UCD in order to provide initial insights to those that aim to endure the same transformation process.* As a next step, we will consolidate such concepts, from literature and practice, into a conceptual model and, in the long run, this conceptual model will be used as the skeleton of a maturity model.

The remainder of this paper presents the mapping between literature and our case study teams' experience, highlighting and discussing the differences between both perspectives.

2   Research Method

We conducted a multiple case study [14] on the two ORG software development teams stationed in our Software Development Lab from April to June, 2019, as presented next.

2.1   Case Setting

ORG has software product development sites in the USA (headquarters), India, and Brazil. With over 7,000 employees and responsible for about 1,200 software products, the IT department started its agile transformation in 2015 and moved to the combined use of Agile, Lean, and UCD principles in late 2017. The adopted approach was inspired by the Pivotal Labs [8] methodology, which proposes a

---

[2] A journal article consolidating the review on the concepts of the 3 approaches and what maturity models are published on the topic is under review, thus we cannot cite it for now. We would like to note that we found no maturity model addressing the 3 approaches together nor for the combination of 2 of them, but we did find 19 models for agile maturity and 5 for lean maturity alone.

[3] We developed an executive report on findings from this study that is of ORG use only. Due to our confidential research agreement with the organization we cannot disclose this document, but we would like to note that there is little on the matter and that what we report in this paper is representative of what is publicly available in blogs, websites, etc of Pivotal customers.

"team rhythm" composed of principles and ceremonies based on the 3 afore-mentioned approaches. It also suggests the adoption of a cross-functional team, called balanced team, composed of three main roles: Product Designer, Product Manager, and Software Engineer. Pivotal Labs' main goal is to help teams to build software products that deliver meaningful value for users and their business. Thus, it offers a framework and initial starting point for any team to discuss its specific needs and define its own way towards software development.

We had two development teams from ORG's Brazilian financial sector stationed in a modern software development lab inside the University's campus. Of the total 16 team members, we interacted with the 8 that participated in a Pivotal hands-on immersion training in the USA. Team A is responsible for a software product that calculates the cost of associated services offered by the products sold by ORG and displays this information to ORG consumers. Team B is responsible for the software product that gathers information about these services from other ORG software products and stores them for Product A to use. These teams spent 3 months in the USA working directly with Pivotal Labs consultants, who played roles in the software development process as hands-on mentors to the ORG members. Afterwards, both teams spent 3 months working at the University's dedicated lab, which is equipped with Pivotal Labs' collaborative work environment recommendations (e.g., single large table for pair-wise work, large screen TV for reports and news, large whiteboards for ideas' development and information sharing, and a meeting room that turns into an entertainment space for leisure time). This last stage is when the data collection and analysis took place.

2.2 Data Collection and Analysis

We used 3 data sources: a questionnaire to collect the participants' profile (name, role, responsibilities, and time working in IT and at ORG); observations to learn about their day to day activities; and focus group sessions to gather information on their perceptions about the transformation, the training experience, the benefits and challenges of the Pivotal Labs approach; and to discuss the concept mapping between literature and what we observed them doing in practice.

Altogether, we performed six focus group sessions that lasted in average 1 hour with the 8 members that worked in the USA. Their profiles are shown in Table 1. Meetings were voice recorded and transcribed for thematic analysis [3,6,18]. Of those six meetings, we used two sessions for each approach. We first presented them the concepts from their practice in order to clarify whether we comprehended them correctly and then we presented the concepts from literature in order to identify the completeness of our observations from practice. By discussing the literature, team members could present us with concepts that we might have missed or misunderstood. We considered the work of Kent Beck [1,2] as literature for XP; Lean Startup [13] and Lean Software Development [12] for Lean; and the work of Norman [11], Brown [4], and Salah, Paige, and Cairns [15] for UCD. We based our definition of literature on existing Pivotal work and an initial observation of the teams. For instance, although Pivotal Labs advocates

Table 1. Participants' profile

ID	Role	Training	IT Work Exp (years)	Company Exp (years)
P1	Software Engineer	Enabler	10	4
P2	Product Manager	Enabler	19	0.5
P3	Product Designer	Enabler	27	10
P4	Software Engineer	Enabler	21	8
P5	Product Manager	Enabler	21	6
P6	Product Designer	Enabler	5	4
P7	Software Engineer	Enabler	20	11
P8	Software Engineer	Enabler	5	5

for the use of Lean Startup (misnaming it as only "Lean"), we observed the use of Lean Software Development concepts, so we decided to consider it as part of the literature for Lean.

3   Results

To facilitate the presentation of the large number of concepts that we identified from literature and later mapped to the case study teams' practice, we introduce these concepts in tables, one per approach (we divided Lean into Lean Startup and Lean Software Development, due to them being radically different). When a concept from literature was not reported by the teams, we indicated "—" in the Case Study table column. Similarly, the concepts identified in practice and lacking in literature are indicated with "—" in the Literature table column. We also organized these concepts into categories, which we name "elements" as per the literature perspective, namely: Activity, Role, Work Product, and Technique/Practice. An exception is the Lean Software Development approach, which organizes itself into Principles that can be realized by Tools, which in turn make use of Concepts as shown in Table 4.

3.1   Extreme Programming

We observed a few differences with our mapping as presented in Table 2. When considering the Activities, the teams put aside their categorization, having them distributed throughout the project life cycle (e.g., BDD as an strategy to validate acceptance tests). With regards to Roles, given that ORG adopted the concept of Balanced Teams from Pivotal Labs, there are three main roles, namely: Product Manager, Product Designer, and Software Engineer. These interchange job responsibilities with XP defined roles, adding them up as stated by some team members: *"The role of Product Designer encompasses more attributions than a Designer"* (P2, P5, P6). A balanced team is described as "a global movement of people who value multidisciplinary collaboration and iterative delivery focused on customer value as a source for innovation" [9]. This concept is used to complement an agile team, as it places the product-focused team members, such as product managers and designers, on equal footing with the team's technical-focused members through a set of core values instead of the definition of explicitly defined roles, events, and artifacts [10]. This allows for a Shared Context. There is also an additional role—Anchor, played by an experienced Software Engineer who, in addition to coding full-time, acts as a resource for the rest of the development team for supporting the resolution of technical and non-technical issues; *"The Anchor role is not necessarily played by the most experienced team member. It is the professional who can talk about the product and about engineering in the same language"* (P1, P2), and *"The Anchor can also be the colleague who will remain in the product team for a longer time, to become a focal point"* (P7). Also, *"The anchor can represent the team in a meeting for clarifications with the user, avoiding the need to send the entire team for this discussion"* (P2). Specific to ORG is the Consultant role, who supports the team, belongs to the Services team, and is responsible for infrastructure and databases.

Considering the Work Products, User Stories can be proposed *"at any time, any role can propose a feature or story"* (P4), however, some members explained that *"We do informally categorize them into Bugs, Features, and Chores"* (P5). *"Bugs are defects that we need to fix, regardless of how they were identified, and Features are new additions to the software product"* (P3). Chores, on the other hand, are a new specialization to indicate that something needs to be done but does not add value to the software: *"We observed some unnecessary processes, in our opinion, and questioned the customers. No one knew what they meant. We just decided alongside with the customers to remove them from the system. We will do this when time allows"* (P7). It is important to note that despite its categorization, all User Stories are now driven by Problem-resolution rather than requirements (as it has been for the past two decades): *"We don't start from the elicitation or clarification of requirements. We now focus on discussing with the customers and users what are the problems they have"* (P8). The Product Backlog is also specialized. The new Ice Box concept is used to indicate User Stories that were either not prioritized yet or were put on hold for some reason, *"Any story can be put on hold in the Ice Box"* (P4), *"We had situations where the business told us that a user story was necessary, but we left it in the Ice Box after realizing it was not relevant. The project evolved and with time the user also realized it was of no use and ended up satisfied with our decision"* (P2). Also, *"We use it as a way to record ideas to avoid forgetting them"* (P4, P8).

When considering the Techniques and Practices, the major mindset change we observed is the fact that the ORG teams do not focus on Releases. They do plan an Iteration as a means to set up expectations with users but they do not estimate efforts or set due dates, *"The term release is used only as a team control mechanism to set the users' expectation and provide visibility"* (P3, P6). This is possible because they are in constant contact with the users, although they

Table 2. Extreme Programming Literature and Case Study Mapping

Literature	Element	Case Study
Coding		Coding
Designing	Activity	—
Testing		—
Listening		Interviews
—		Anchor
Consultant		Services Consultant
Coach		Product Manager
Tester		Product Designer/Software Engineer
Programmer	Role	Software Engineer
Tracker		Software Engineer
Manager		Product Manager
Doomsayer		Product Manager
Big Boss		Product Manager
Customer		Product Manager
Bug Fix		Bug
User Story	Work Product	Problem-based User Story — Feature / Chore
Product Backlog		Product Backlog — Current / Ice Box
Iteration Backlog		—
Release Planning		—
Iteration Planning		Pre-Iteration Planning Meeting (Pre-IPM)/ Iteration Planning Meeting (IPM)
Customer Approval		User Feedback
Pair Programming		Pair Programming
Acceptance Test-Driven Development		—
Test-Driven Development		Test-Driven Development
Customer Tests/ On-Site Customer		—
Continuous Delivery		Continuous Delivery
Refactoring/ Design Improvement		Refactoring
Continuous Integration		Continuous Integration
Planning Game		Planning Game
Estimation by Example		—
—		Behavior-Driven Development (BDD)
Spike		Experiments
Daily Meeting	Technique/ Practice	Daily Stand-Up
Stand-up Meeting		Office Stand-up/Team Stand-up
Whole Team		Balanced Team
Collective Ownership/ Collective Code Ownership		Collective Ownership
Coding Standards		S.O.L.I.D.
40 Hours per Week/Sustainable Pace		Sustainable Pace
Constant Feedback		Constant Feedback
Simple Design		Simple Design
Metaphor		Metaphor
Small Releases		Small Increments
Retrospective		Retrospective
—		Tech Talks
—		Shared Context
—		Team Agreement
—		Question Actual Process
—		Information Repository

are not On-Site Customers but *"they are nearby"* (P1). They also believe that a good way to constantly collect User Feedback is by using BDD: *"We use BDD to have better communication with our users. We validate our acceptance tests, which in turn validate the users' perspectives"* (P5). Spikes, simple programs to explore potential solutions, often not good enough to keep, are used in a slightly different way than proposed in literature. The ORG teams use spikes as a resource for their experimentation of hypotheses, *"We work up to 4 hours if needed to build a spike to experiment our theories and explore possibilities"* (P2).

Other smalls adjustments to concepts from literature are: instead of only writing code in accordance with rules (Coding Standards), the teams use SOLID, the mnemonic acronym for five design principles intended to make software designs more understandable, flexible, and maintainable—Single responsibility, Open–closed, Liskov substitution, Interface segregation, and Dependency inversion principle. Tech Talks meetings focus on exposing a subject of interest to the teams and other colleagues who want to learn something new. These meetings can be of technical nature or comprise any other aspect. Team Agreement refers to any kind of decision the team makes that will take longer than 30 min to be implemented and therefore is worth discussing and recording. Question Actual Process is the mindset *"we learned from Pivotal; they instigated us to be investigative all the time by asking questions when we see fit"* (P2, P5). And, finally, Information Repository is used as a resource to maintain a shared context *"where everyone has access to information about the problems we are trying to resolve. Currently we are using Slack to make it easier"* (P3, P6).

3.2   Lean

Lean Startup. Overall, we identified that the Lean Startup (LS) concepts used by the ORG teams are all heavily centered around conducting experiments, as stated by a Software Engineer, *"Let's conduct an experiment to validate if this approach will be better. If it works, let's proceed. How do we know this? Through experimentation."* (P7), and being able to make informed decisions, as exemplified by a Product Manager: *"The team compiled the results and sent them to the stakeholders saying: 'look, these are the results and this is what we've learned. What are we going to do with it? Do you want to follow this approach or the other one? The decision is yours.'"* (P2).

As part of the Activity element, we find some activities related to LS principles, e.g., Building Experiments, Measuring Results, and Learning being directly associated with the Build Measure Learn Cycle. A similar phenomenon happens in the Work Product section, where Iterate, Escalate, Persevere, and Give Up are outcomes of the principle Validated Learning. The 31 techniques presented in Table 3 were extracted from the Lean Startup book by Eric Ries [13].

We found that ORG teams use a subset of the activities mapped from the literature. The core experimentation cycle activities related to the principles of Build Measure Learn and Innovation Accounting are used normally, however Formulating the Business Model and Hypotheses is approached in a different

Table 3. Lean Startup Literature and Case Study Mapping

Literature		Element	Case Study	
Formulating the Business Model and Hypotheses		Activity	Understanding the Problem	
			Defining the Team's Vision of the Problem	
			Establishing the Team's Strategy to Solve the Problem	
			Mapping Everyone Affected by the Problem (Users and Stakeholders)	
			Formulating Hypotheses	
Build Measure Learn (Principle)	Building Experiments		Build Measure Learn (Principle)	Building Experiments
	Measuring Results			Measuring Results
	Learning			Learning
Innovation Accounting (Principle)	Establish the Baseline		Innovation Accounting (Principle)	Establish the Baseline
	Tune the Engine			Tune the Engine
	Pivot or Persevere			Pivot or Persevere
Running the Engine of Growth			—	
Pivot or Persevere Meeting			—	
Entrepreneur		Role	Team	
Ideas (Hypotheses)		Work Product	Ideas (Hypotheses)	
Product			Product	
Data (Metrics and Measurements)			Data (Metrics and Measurements)	
Validated Learning (Principle)	Iterate		Validated Learning (Principle)	Iterate
	Escalate			—
	Persevere			Persevere
	Give Up			Give Up
	—			Double Down
Split Tests		Technique / Practice	—	
Small Batches			Small Batches	
Triple "A" Metrics (Actionable, Accessible, Auditable)			—	
Customer Development			Customer Development	
5 Whys			5 Whys	
Customer Advisory Board			—	
Falsifiable Hypotheses			—	
Product Owner			—	
Accountability			—	
Customer Archetypes			Customer Archetypes	
Cross-Functional Teams			Balanced Teams	
Smoke Tests			—	
Continuous Deployment			Continuous Deployment	
Usability Tests			—	
Real-Time Monitoring & Alerting			Real-Time Monitoring & Alerting	
Customer Liaison			Customer Liaison	
Funnel Analysis			—	
Cohort Analysis			—	
Net Promoter Score			—	
Search Engine Marketing			—	
Predictive Monitoring			—	
Unit Tests			Unit Tests	
Continuous Integration			Continuous Integration	
Incremental Deployment			Incremental Deployment	
Free & Open-Source			—	
Cloud Computing			—	
Cluster Immune System			—	
Just-In-Time Scalability			—	
Refactoring			Refactoring	
Developer Sandbox			—	
Minimum Viable Product			Minimum Viable Product	

way, since the team's goal is to solve the company's problems instead of creating a sustainable business: the team focuses on understanding the problem at hand, so that they can build a common understanding and a strategy to tackle it. A Product Manager says: *"When we are identifying a problem, we contact the stakeholders in order to understand what the problem we're dealing with is. We spent the whole morning discussing everything we thought was related to the problem, and everything that could be a problem, until we reached a final statement. After that, as a team, we defined the vision and the strategy that we were going to use to solve the problem. . . "* (P2). We did not identify the explicit usage of <u>Pivot or Persevere Meetings</u> and <u>Engines of Growth</u>.

We did not identify any explicit categorization of roles in the literature. Eric Ries often refers to the ones conducting the scientific method of the LS as <u>Entrepreneurs</u>. In our case study, this role is taken by the <u>Team</u> as a whole.

Regarding Work Products, the main difference found is that the teams did not mention <u>Escalate</u> as an informed decision based on the outcome of an experiment, i.e., a <u>Validated Learning</u> outcome. A Software Engineer says that *"The decisions normally are: you can abandon that track of work; you can persevere, and continue to work on that; you can pivot, change the direction and try to investigate it in another way; or you can even double down on it, things are going the right way but we want it to go faster, so we put more engineers to work on it."* (P4) Among the 31 presented Techniques, we identified that the team actively uses 13 of them. Most notably, we found that the concept of <u>Cross-functional Teams</u> is mapped to <u>Balanced Teams</u>, as previously mentioned in the XP approach (Sect. 3.1).

Lean Software Development. Most of what is presented by the Poppendiecks [12] is used in some way by the ORG development teams as seen in Table 4. We observed that the <u>Iteration</u> tool is used differently: ORG teams disregard the use of *fixed time-boxes*, as *"[stakeholders do not impose deadlines], unless there's a compliance or interlocking deadline already in-place"* (P5), although a Software Engineer adds that *"stakeholders have target dates or launch windows for the final solution, and we aim to deliver it all by then"* (P4). Additionally, Iterations have an open scope, says a Software Engineer: *"We might have decided to work on two User Stories for a given Iteration, but if something—anything—comes up mid-iteration, we reshuffle our priorities and work on something else"* (P8).

For <u>Synchronization</u> purposes, the teams prefer the use of *spanning application* instead of *matrix*: upon being asked if they develop a system by sketching out its components and then splitting the team to work on each, a Software Engineer responded, *"No, we make experiments—a whole slice of a solution, comprised of the full technology stack, to see if it works. If it does, we expand upon it"* (P4). In regards to the team's decision making process (<u>Making Decisions</u>), all decisions are made exclusively through the interpretation of experiment results, disregarding the Poppendiecks' *intuitive decision making* and *simple rules* (we called this *experiment-based decisions*). Although an expert's intuition can influence the decision or open up more options, the final say comes from experimentation, as stated by a Software Engineer: *"We needed to insert a lot of data into a database, and it was taking too long with our current technology stack. I developed a solution using another technology stack that I was sure was going to perform better. As I thought, it did, so we started using it"* (P1).

Table 4. Lean Software Development Literature and Case Study Mapping

Literature			Case Study		
Principle	**Tool**	**Concept**	**Principle**	**Tool**	**Concept**
Eliminate Waste	Seeing Waste		Eliminate Waste	Seeing Waste	
	Value Stream Mapping			Value Stream Mapping	
Amplify Learning	Feedback		Amplify Learning	Feedback	
	Iteration	Negotiable Scope		Iteration	Negotiable Scope
		Team Commitment			Team Commitment
		Fixed Time-Box			—
	Set-Based Development	Constraints		Set-Based Development	Constraints
		Multiple Options			Multiple Options
	Synchronization	Daily Build and Smoke Test		Synchronization	Daily Build and Smoke Test
		Spanning Application			Spanning Application
		Matrix			—
Decide as Late as Possible	Making Decisions	Intuitive Decision Making	Decide as Late as Possible	Making Decisions	—
		Simple Rules			—
		—			Experiment-Based
	Options Thinking			Options Thinking	
	The Last Responsible Moment			The Last Responsible Moment	
Deliver as Fast as Possible	Cost of Delay	Economic Model	Deliver as Fast as Possible	Cost of Delay	Economic Model
	Pull Systems	Information Radiators		Pull Systems	Information Radiators
	Queueing Theory	Small Work Packages		Queueing Theory	Small Work Packages
		Slack			Slack
		Steady Rate of Service			Steady Rate of Service
		Steady Rate of Arrival			Steady Rate of Arrival
Empower the Team	Expertise	Communities of Expertise	Empower the Team	Expertise	Communities of Expertise
		Standards			Standards
	Motivation	Belonging, Safety, Competence, and Progress		Motivation	Belonging, Safety, Competence, and Progress
		Moderation			Moderation
		Purpose			Purpose
		Champion			—
	Self-Determination	Principles, Not Practices		Self-Determination	Principles, Not Practices
	Leadership	Master Developer		—	
Build Integrity In	Conceptual Integrity	Software Architecture	Build Integrity In	Conceptual Integrity	Software Architecture
	Perceived Integrity	Institutional Memory		Perceived Integrity	Institutional Memory
		Model-Driven Design			Model-Driven Design
	Refactoring			Refactoring	
	Testing	As-Built Test Suite		Testing	As-Built Test Suite
		Customer Tests			Customer Tests
		Developer Tests			Developer Tests
See the Whole	Measurements	Information Measurement	See the Whole	Measurements	Information Measurement
	Contracts	Target-Cost Contracts		—	
		Time-And-Material Contracts			
		Shared-Benefit Contracts			
		Multistage Contracts			

Concerning Motivation, ORG teams do not have a *champion*, a person that compels other members to work on a project. Instead, they all compel themselves to work, as stated by a Software Engineer: *"The empathy we feel for our work colleagues motivates us to work"* (P1). As for Leadership, we observed that the ORG teams do not have leaders at all: a Software Engineer points out that each role in the Balanced Team spearheads its respective domain (e.g., Software Engineers lead technical discussions), but also adds that *"all decisions are shared and made by the whole team"* (P4), while a Product Manager emphasizes that *"[even a rookie can make] the most experienced team member say 'You are right, let's do it your way.'"* (P2). Finally, ORG teams dismiss the need for Contracts since they work for ORG itself: *"We do not sign any legal contracts. ORG decides what problems need solving, and these eventually trickle down to us"* (P2).

3.3   User-Centered Design

Table 5 shows the *Phases*, *Activities*, *Work Products*, and *Techniques* for UCD. The Phases, shown in the left side of the activities in the table, from literature, are related to the Double Diamond of *Design Thinking*. The idea is to perform the UCD activities inside of the *Finding the Problem* and *Finding the Solution* phases [11]. It is important to mention that we identified 77 techniques from the literature, however, Table 5 shows only the most cited techniques and those identified in our case study.

We found that the phases and activities of the UCD literature are the same used by the teams. In terms of Phases, the difference is the used terminology. We identified the *Finding the Problem* phase is the *Discovery* phase and the *Finding Solution* is the *Framing* phase. For the Activities, the first difference was in the *Testing* activity that originally (from literature) focus on validating the solution with the final users. In the studied teams, the solution is validated internally by the Product Designer (PD) and Product Manager (PM) roles in the *Seek Feedback* activity before being validated with the final users: *"The PM and PD will validate if the solution proposed is according to what was developed by the team. PM and PD validate before reaching the user. They will either accept or reject the story"* (P4); *"Sometimes we do not even have access to the user"* (P7). Another difference in terms of activities was that the teams perform an additional activity named *Communicate Early and Often*. This activity is related to the designer's pairing with the team members during product development: *"During implementation, the PD can pair with an engineer to ensure that this engineer has all the understanding he needs to develop"* (P4), *"It is the responsibility of the whole team to deliver the correct product"* (P5).

As for UCD Work Products and Roles, we did not observe any differences between those used in the team and the literature. The teams have the role *Product Designer* and produce a small set of work products connected with the applied techniques by them. Finally, we identify that of the 77 UCD techniques listed in literature, the teams have only used 7 of them so far. They also used 4 techniques we had not found in literature. Indeed, what we could obverse was that although they did not use a vast amount of techniques,

Table 5. User-Centered Design Literature and Case Study Mapping

Literature	Element	Case Study
Finding the Problem and Finding the Solution Phases — Observation/Inspiration	Activity — Discovery and Framing Phases	Conduct Research
Ideation		Generate Solutions
Prototyping		Deliver Design Decisions
Testing		Seek Feedback
		Testing
—		Communicate Early and Often
Designer	**Role**	Product Designer
Prototype	**Work Product**	Prototype
User Journey Map		—
Business Model Canvas		—
Scenarios		—
Stakeholders Mapping		—
Persona		Persona
Affinity Diagram		Affinity Mapping
Blueprint		Blueprint
Photo Journal		—
Empathy Mapping		—
Mind Mapping		—
Storytelling		—
Card Sorting		—
Prototyping		Prototyping
Ethnography		—
Interview	**Technique / Practice**	Interview
Brainstorming		Design Session
5 Why		—
Point of View		—
Questionnaire		—
Usability Test		—
Inspection		—
Profiles		—
Survey		—
How Might We		How Might We
—		2x2 Prioritization
—		Now, Near, Next
—		Integration Research
—		Design Studio

they are continually searching and studying new techniques, as argued by a Product Manager, *"Techniques are things that we keep looking for, studying, and eventually applying"* (P5). The teams pointed out *How Might We* and *2 × 2 Prioritization* as the most used techniques: *"How Might We is one that we use a lot"* (P6). *"We always use How Might We because it helps us think about the value that solution will deliver"* (P5). Concerning *2 × 2 Prioritization* they said: *"2 × 2 to identify the pain points"* (P3), *"2 × 2 can be used in prob-*

lems, solutions" (P5), *"2 × 2 to validate with user"* (P4), and *"2 × 2 is used as wild card"* (P7). They also mentioned the *Product Designer* as responsible for choosing better techniques for each situation: *"The Product Designer has the responsibility to attempt to identify the best technique to validate as fast as possible the teams' assumptions. The Product Designer tries to find the better technique to validate the idea"* (P6).

4   Discussion

Evolution is natural for software development with the adoption of new methodologies and technologies—the evolution of XP with the joint use of other approaches in the industry is evidenced in our research. The shared responsibilities, resulting of the multidisciplinary work, is a valid direction with increasing complexity in software development. More specifically, a balanced team works with no time-bound iterations (no Iteration Planning) as a mean to continuously deliver value to the customer. To do so, the main mindset change is to now focus on problems (Problem-based User Stories) rather than on requirements as the starting point of customer interaction and involvement.

As for Lean, the ORG teams seem to use a subset of LS and LSD that complements the use of one another. For instance, the teams' Decision Making does not use the concepts provided by LSD, instead, it uses *experiment-based decisions*, which is completely rooted in LS. Following this example is the lack of Leadership: since all decisions are experiment-driven, there is no need for a leader or boss figure among the team.

In regards to UCD, it seems that both teams only use a subset of its available tools, and understandably so, given how many of them there are. Not only that, but each team uses different sets of tools for their respective problems, indicating that there is really no be-all-end-all tool package to product design.

As a side note, we observed that both teams always seek to adapt techniques, practices, and roles to their context: they seem to have a "drive" to strive for the best way to do their jobs at all times. We believe this is a good indicator for the undergoing transformation of ORG. This also leads us to leave the following questions up in the air: are the differences identified in our mapping an issue? Since teams are always evolving, can our study be a good-to-have-at-hand document for consulting?

5   Final Considerations

As part of a long-term research project that aims to define a maturity model to help teams in their transformation to the combined use of XP, Lean, and UCD, we report in this paper our first step: the mapping between the identified underlying concepts from literature and those used by the observed ORG teams. From the comparison between the results from literature and our case study with the two teams that have been undergoing this transformation process for about 6 months, we found that the teams' use of Pivotal Labs is mostly aligned with the literature, but differs in some aspects, namely:

- All decisions are based on experiments, disregarding the intuition of experts;
- Lack of leaders, since the team inspires itself and shares decision making equally;
- There is an Anchor role, that bridges the understanding between business and engineering;
- Not all UCD techniques are used, but the teams are constantly seeking out to use new ones that might benefit their case.

This initial contribution can already be of use to software development teams aiming to endure such transformation. By revealing the concepts from literature, practitioners can have a broad overview of what they might have to deliberate on and can use, and by identifying what is being used by a maturing team that has been experiencing such transformation as part of a large multinational IT company, practitioners can envision some adjustments that have been proven to work so far. We note that our results are not generalizable nor are conclusive given the exploratory nature of our case study. However, they are a first step towards our main goal. We will continue observing other teams (there are 4 teams confirmed for the coming 6 months) in the University lab and contacting the past observed teams every 3 months as a means to identify how they mature throughout time. We expected to soon report on our to-be-proposed maturity model.

Acknowledgement. We would like to thank the study participants from ORG. Also, we thank ORG for the financial support (Brazilian Informatics Law n° 8.2.48 of 1991).

References

1. Beck, K.: Embracing change with extreme programming. Computer **32**(10), 70–77 (1999). https://doi.org/10.1109/2.796139
2. Beck, K., Andres, C.: Extreme Programming Explained: Embrace Change, 2nd edn. Addison-Wesley, Upper Saddle River (2004)
3. Braun, V., Clarke, V.: Using thematic analysis in psychology. Qual. Res. Psychol. **3**(2), 77–101 (2006). https://doi.org/10.1191/1478088706qp063oa. https://www.tandfonline.com/doi/pdf/10.1191/1478088706qp063oa. https://www.tandfonline.com/doi/abs/10.1191/1478088706qp063oa
4. Brown, T.: Design thinking. Harvard Bus. Rev. **86**, 84–92, 141 (2008)
5. Dobrigkeit, F., de Paula, D., Uflacker, M.: InnoDev: a software development methodology integrating design thinking, scrum and lean startup. In: Meinel, C., Leifer, L. (eds.) Design Thinking Research. UI, pp. 199–227. Springer, Cham (2019). https://doi.org/10.1007/978-3-319-97082-0_11
6. Gregory, P., Barroca, L., Taylor, K., Salah, D., Sharp, H.: Agile challenges in practice: a thematic analysis. In: Lassenius, C., Dingsøyr, T., Paasivaara, M. (eds.) XP 2015. LNBIP, vol. 212, pp. 64–80. Springer, Cham (2015). https://doi.org/10.1007/978-3-319-18612-2_6
7. Grossman-Kahn, B., Rosensweig, R.: Skip the silver bullet: driving innovation through small bets and diverse practices. In: Leading Through Design, p. 815 (2012)

8. Pivotal Software Inc.: Pivotal Labs (2019). https://pivotal.io/labs. Accessed 18 July 2019
9. Jarrell, J., Berner, I.: Balanced Team: A Balanced Approach to Product Design and Delivery (2014). http://www.balancedteam.org/. Accessed 18 July 2019
10. Jarrell, J., Berner, I.: Striking the Right Balance with Balanced Teams (2019). https://content.pivotal.io/white-papers/striking-the-right-balance-with-balanced-teams. Accessed 18 July 2019
11. Norman, D.A.: The Design of Everyday Things. Basic Books, New York (2002)
12. Poppendieck, M., Poppendieck, T.: Lean Software Development: An Agile Toolkit. Addison-Wesley, Boston (2003)
13. Ries, E.: The Lean Startup: How Today's Entrepreneurs Use Continuous Innovation to Create Radically Successful Businesses. Crown Business, New York (2011)
14. Runeson, P., Höst, M.: Guidelines for conducting and reporting case study research in software engineering. Empirical Softw. Eng. **14**(2), 131 (2008). https://doi.org/10.1007/s10664-008-9102-8
15. Salah, D., Paige, R.F., Cairns, P.: A systematic literature review for agile development processes and user centred design integration. In: Proceedings of the 18th International Conference on Evaluation and Assessment in Software Engineering, London, England, pp. 5:1–5:10. ACM (2014). https://doi.org/10.1145/2601248.2601276
16. Sedano, T.: Sustainable Software Development: Evolving Extreme Programming, April 2017. https://doi.org/10.1184/R1/6723431.v1. https://kilthub.cmu.edu/articles/Sustainable_Software_Development_Evolving_Extreme_Programming/6723431
17. Sedano, T., Ralph, P., Péraire, C.: Sustainable software development through overlapping pair rotation. In: Proceedings of the 10th ACM/IEEE International Symposium on Empirical Software Engineering and Measurement, ESEM 2016, Ciudad Real, Spain, pp. 19:1–19:10. ACM (2016). https://doi.org/10.1145/2961111.2962590
18. Vaismoradi, M., Turunen, H., Bondas, T.: Content analysis and thematic analysis: implications for conducting a qualitative descriptive study. Nurs. Health Sci. **15**(3), 398–405 (2013). https://doi.org/10.1111/nhs.12048. https://onlinelibrary.wiley.com/doi/pdf/10.1111/nhs.12048. https://onlinelibrary.wiley.com/doi/abs/10.1111/nhs.12048
19. Ximenes, B.H., Alves, I.N., Araújo, C.C.: Software project management combining agile, lean startup and design thinking. In: Marcus, A. (ed.) DUXU 2015. LNCS, vol. 9186, pp. 356–367. Springer, Cham (2015). https://doi.org/10.1007/978-3-319-20886-2_34

Mob Programming and Simultaneous Style Pair Programming in the Development of a Battle Royale Game: An Action Research

Herez Moise Kattan$^{(\boxtimes)}$

Department of Computer Science, Institute of Mathematics and Statistics
of the University of Sao Paulo (IME-USP), Sao Paulo, Sao Paulo, Brazil
`Herez@ime.usp.br`, `Herez@Herez.com.br`, `Herez@acm.org`
`https://www.Herez.com.br`

Abstract. This paper is an Action Research about adopting Mob Programming and Simultaneous Style Pair Programming to develop a battle royale game called Pirate Ship Battles. Mob Programming helps the developers to learn an open-source framework for games called Phaser and another one called Jest to automatization of the tests. The following are two examples of insights that occurred respectively in the first and third cycles of action research. The team collaboratively agreed to start by learning in a Mob Programming doing the infra-structure to the tests and also to deepen the knowledge about Phaser should help in the next parts of the project. Another example of insight occurred in the third cycle of this action research is about testing activity, fixing the bugs, was observed funnier comparing with testing alone. The team reported it was funnier testing altogether, when a mistake happens to run new code, everybody paying attention to the projector on the fault, a ready joke. Perhaps, because they are friends and the project is a game. Another possible explanation about our experience of funnier testing activity in a Mob Programming compared to testing alone is that we humans are social beings. Concluding, the source code of the game is of excellent quality as evaluated by CodeClimate by classifying it with grade A, the developers enjoyed, and both approaches increased the learnings.

Keywords: Collaboration in software development · Agile practice ·
Programming teams · Programming technique · Mob Programming ·
Pair Programming · Simultaneous Style Pair Programming ·
Collaborative problem solving · Social-technical system · Action
research

1 Introduction

Nowadays, the number of new technologies need to develop modern software is very high. There are early adopters of these new practices of Mob Programming

© Springer Nature Switzerland AG 2019
P. Meirelles et al. (Eds.): WBMA 2019, CCIS 1106, pp. 41–57, 2019.
https://doi.org/10.1007/978-3-030-36701-5_4

and Simultaneous Style Pair Programming. However, to increase the number of organizations investing in the creation of software accepting try to use them, requires an impartial evaluation of the potential beneficial practices with a scientific research method. Toward to adopt these software development practices with more confident, this is important for them, because of understanding better when using these new practices and exactly how the best way.

The motivation of the present work starts from the premise that software development is a socio-technical system in which people develop software based on technological tools. Collaboration among people is a relevant aspect, as well as the interaction with the technical/technological tools involved in the process of software development [19, 21, 24].

Socio-technical systems consist of social and technical/technological systems. Both parts could be optimized together or not. In other words, they may or may not have been designed to ensure both systems contributing together to the best possible human and organizational results [2].

Mob Programming is a software system development and testing technique in which programmers sit side by side, all together around the same computer. This approach of programming all together exercises social aspects due programmers are working on the same activity, looking at the same projector, sharing the keyboard and mouse, making the programming activity much more social with intense collaboration and constant communication [20].

The **goal** of this paper is to programming a game using social computing in the form of open science, describing it here through action research its creation process. The team uses *Mob Programming* and Simultaneous Style Pair Programming, all the interviews about the development of the game with its source code as *open source* are for free on GitHub and Wiki. The game is a Socio-Technical system because beyond its technological part has a social one to play online on the internet. It is mandatorily a *multiplayer*, to make sense it is necessary another person also enters in WebSite, login, and play with at least one other player. The game becomes more fun the more players there are. Placing the game on GitHub is also for a socio-technical reason to encourage other developers to collaborate with the technical part, helping in their programming, both functional and corrective evolutions.

Action Research is a collaborative research method. In which, the members of the studied system participate actively in a cycle of planning activities, taking action, and evaluation of results. This research method was a natural choice, me being part of the game development team. Follow is a description of insight happened in the first cycle of action research.

Plan: the game is of the genre battle royale, so, we will need to program a circle of death. Thus, this rule of the game is about the player suffering damage if out that circle and making the player lose their life in the game every few seconds. We also need to create a scoreboard and one a minimap.

Act: we split into two groups of Mob Programming. The first was composed of three people Mob programming the circle of death and the second creating the scoreboard and minimap.

Observe: because of the level of difficulty of programming a circle of death with many visual effects involved, we observed that Mob Programming was helpful to do it.

Reflect: one possible reason to be a positive approach is because of the complexity of the task. Another consideration is the learning need for use by the first time o the framework 'Phaser' 3.0 for our team.

The team faced some challenges with the adoption of Mob Programming. We need a room with a good projector, tables, and chairs. We need previously reserve them exclusively for us and I that was also the coach of the team spent some time doing this negotiation. We had a short deadline and a lot of features to deliver, so, we decide and need, combine Mob Programming with Pair Programming and Simultaneous Style Pair Programming. For this last challenge, I explain in this paper some outcomes about design, user stories adaptation, and software requirements related to this.

Now, we have a playable game. Would be amazing to get more contributors to work with us to improve the game toward making it a commercial success. I am trying to do it as an open science project. All the audios of the interviews, the source code, the metrics, and data are available in our Wiki and GitHub.

Following are the Background need to fulfill understanding of this paper, the Research Method description, Literature Review, the cycles of the Action Research, Limitations, and Conclusion.

2   Background

The following sections presents the introductions about socio-technical systems, mob programming, and background knowledge need to a clear understanding of this paper.

2.1   Socio-Technical Systems

The Socio-Technical Systems theory mentioned in the introduction to this article originated in the Institute Tavistock. The researchers who created it believed it was an advance in the design of the organizations to be more suitable for people working.

Socio-Technical Systems has had an impact around the world for more than 50 years, so we can consider it to be a much more successful theory rather than most organizational theories [1]. Eason used the metaphor of a half-empty glass, and he published in 2008 his metaphor and was particularly appropriate for Socio-Technical Systems theory at that time, an approach with enormous potential, however, it was only partially realized [1].

I agree with the potential on Socio-Technical systems, so, I analyze here some potentially useful aspects for the organization of the work of the programmers. The scope of this work is aspects useful related to Mob Programming or getting deep the understanding of the practice and its popularity among programmers when they begin to practice. In this endeavor, the state-of-the-art will deepen the knowledge about this new software development practice.

The way people organize to work collaboratively with common or shared ends continues to interest scientists, academics, and leaders in general. Cooperative work is essential in microenterprises, also in the start-up phase, medium and large governmental and non-governmental organizations.

Because the world is continually changing around us, it forces people and organizations to look for new ways to work together to change and adapt. This is increasingly important in the globalized service economy. We are currently facing global challenges that affect our lives. At the same time, there is a greater focus on innovation as people try to solve these problems. New organizational structures arise to support entrepreneurship and new forms of work. Thus, the concepts originally developed at the Tavistock Institute seem quite relevant and offer possible solutions for the present day [2].

2.2 Mob Programming

The idea of Mob Programming originated from developer lunch meetings in a presentation format, where a team member presented a code he knew [6]. Mob programming is a technique where the entire team participates around a workstation with a single person in possession of the keyboard, mouse, and computer [7,9].

A study of Mob Programming observed that in moments of doubt when no team member has sufficient technical knowledge about the current issue, it is best to separate the group and continue the work simultaneously [19,20]. Figure 1 illustrates the basic workspace setup of Mob Programming.

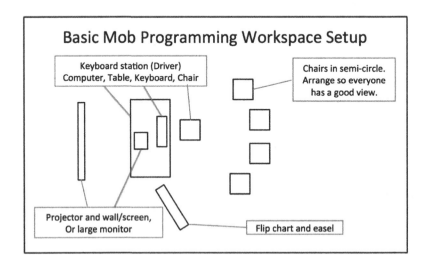

Fig. 1. The basic setup of Mob Programming by Zuil et al. [9].

2.3   Simultaneous Style Pair Programming

A possibility to increase the productivity of pair programming is to use the parallelism of Concurrent Engineering [15]. Another alternative is the incorporation of a process of pair code review.

According to Coplien et al. [14], the design is compatible with the pairing of working together. In this way, they can produce more than the sum of the two individually.

Figure 2 illustrates the basic workflow of the Simultaneous Style Pair Programming excluding the Planning phase and the Rest phase because are very difficult to draw.

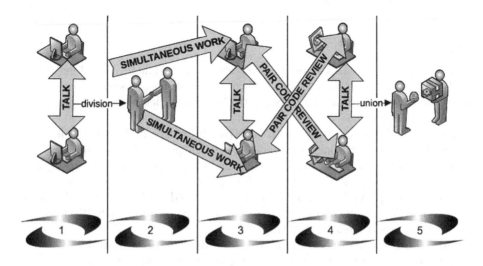

Fig. 2. The basic workflow of the Simultaneous Style Pair Programming.

The Programming and Review Simultaneous in Pairs (PrsP): a pair programming extension of Kattan [16] is also known as Simultaneous Style Pair Programming [25] or as Pair Development. PrsP has the following definition:

"A programming activity wherein planning is at the beginning including the pair selection, the pairing of tasks is collaboratively designed and based on these two programmers work collaboratively in the same activity. Only in the beginning of one activity sitting side by side to exchange experiences (this way there are more algorithms and solutions) or communicate in the beginning, if they are working in a distributed way (different locations). Still, in this initial phase, they decide how to divide the task, and do not need to sit together all the time on a single computer, or communicate at all times if they are working in a distributed way, only when necessary and useful. Whenever possible, the work should be performed simultaneously on separate computers. Unlike traditional pair programming, in PrsP each programmer revises the work of the other one simultaneously using two computers if an error is found then the task returns to the programmer fix it. In the end, they unite the work of the pair. During the rest, it is suggested to speak or to think about the best way for the accomplishment of the work, mindset zero defect, adoption of a process of stress reduction and for resolution of conflicts" [16,25].

2.4   Social Computing

The internet has brought a different style of computing because it is dependent on human interactions. Even the success of program execution often depends on the properties of the human society in which the programmed software system is inserted, as it is being operated by humans [5].

2.5   Action Research

In the late 1930s, Kurt Lewin and his students researched factories and neighborhoods to demonstrate respectively higher productivity gains as well as employee rights and order in the workplace respectively through democratic participation in autocratic coercion.

Lewin, in addition to showing an effective alternative to Taylor and his Scientific Management, through his Action Research provided the details of how to develop social relations of groups and between groups to support communication and cooperation. To achieve such conditions and required relationships, forms of leadership very different from those provided by Taylor's literal followers and Tyler's misinterpretation which led to a connection with Watsonian's 'behaviorism' and therefore objectivist [3].

One of the summaries on forms of leadership was made by two of Lewin's former students, named Cartwright and Zander [4]. Action research was the systematic research method used for all participants to seek greater effectiveness together through democratic participation. Following is the detailing of the research method used.

3   Research Method

Justifying the choice to do an action-research: perhaps because Mob Programming is a way of organizing the work of group programmers, and action research has its origins as described above in working groups, it helps to explain such similarity between Lewin's research and his the students we are doing here.

Of course with the difference that our workgroup is composed of programmers while Lewis and his students research with a group of factory workers. Just as in Lewin's time we believe it to be a suitable research method to study the social aspects involved in the work of a group, in our case, specifically of programmers. Thus, we chose Action Research as a research method for the work reported here.

Action research is a collaborative research method in which members of the studied system actively participate in a cycle of planning, action, and outcome evaluation activities [10]. This action research is part of a project including a extensive literature review [19]. Often research methods can be used as a combination and toward make this contribution stronger, there are others papers related following a mixed method called illuminated arrow [17,18].

The history of socio-technical systems is closely linked to action research. This is more of a philosophy than a methodology. It describes a humanistic process and set of principles that in our context is associated with technology and change. It can be used to contribute to most problem solutions in work situations, as long as both innovators and recipients are willing to use a democratic approach. It will be difficult to use it successfully if the parties involved are hostile to each other, disinterested in developing strategies and unwilling or unable to co-operate. As the name implies, the research approach has an action component: either the research is intended to lead to changes in the work situation or produces an inadvertent change because action research has occurred [11].

Action research according with my experience is a way of making a systematic process for collective reflection in social situations toward improving rationality and justice by those who are involved in the process as well as understanding by those involved and in the situations studied.

Action research is a form of collective self-reflexive research conducted by participants in social situations to improve the rationality and justice of their own social or educational practices, as well as the understanding of those practices and situations in which practices are performed [12].

According to Rose et al., Although some variant of the? Plan-act-observe-reflect? The cycle is at the core of most studies that use action research, the precise form depends on the approach chosen and the objectives of each search [13].

Figure 3 illustrates the spiral concerning the process of collective reflection in terms of its cycles of **plan-act-observe-reflect**.

The Fig. 3 is by Kemmis et al. [12] and it illustrates the spiral of self-reflection in terms of a spiral of self-reflective cycles of:

- **Planning** a change,
- **Action** and **Observation** of the process and its consequences of the change,
- **Reflection** on these processes and their consequences, and then
- **Replanning** of items,
- **Act** again and **Observe** again,
- **Reflection** about these processes and their consequences,
- **and so on...** (see Fig. 3)

The following are the action-research cycles occurred during the development of the Socio-Technical game. Afterward, it is the analysis of results. In the end, the conclusions are presented, summarizing the main findings.

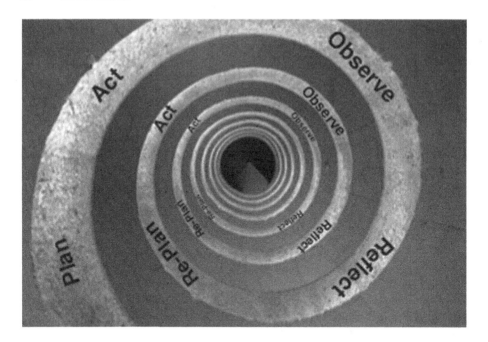

Fig. 3. The Research-Action spiral is by Kemmis et al. [12] and it illustrates the spiral of self-reflection in terms of a spiral of self-reflective cycles of **plan-act-observe-reflect-replanning-act-observe-reflect-and so on**.

4 Battle Royale Style Game Called *Pirate Ship Battles*

This section describes the cycles of action research during the development of a *Battle Royale* game. This research was carried out during the second half of 2018 in the disciplines XP Laboratory (LabXP) and Advanced Laboratory of Agile Methods of the Department of Computer Science of the Institute of Mathematics and Statistics of the University of Sao Paulo (IME-USP). The students of the disciplines were the developers of this game with a Socio-Technical aspect, *multiplayer online* in which to be entertaining it takes more than one player.

Since Agile Methods formalization, the software engineering education has also been impacted with universities adapting their courses as a way to suit this new software processes. At the University of Sao Paulo (USP), there is a discipline called XP Laboratory (LabXP). Although the name refers to eXtreme Programming, the discipline aims at teaching agile methods in practice, considering several elements that are crucial for providing the student with real knowledge and experience with agile methods. This discipline has provided extensive studies involving students, instructors, mentors, customers, professionals, and companies [8].

The course requires a minimum of at least eight hours per week of dedication, and there is a lunch once a week, to allow the students to share experiences. First, the teams watched a workshop about Mob Programming and Simultaneous Style

Pair Programming with Herez Moise Kattan, the author was also a developer and coach of the team. All the data are open source. An interview was done to deepen the knowledge about the experience of the team members.

4.1   Context

The client requesting the game was a university extension group of the IME-USP called University of Sao Paulo group for game development (USPGAMEDEV). This group is composed of students and non-students of the university. It is focused exclusively for the development of games.

The Socio-Technical game has the requirement of being developed with continuous integration and automated tests. *Pirate Ship Battles* is a 2D open-source game of the genre *battle royale*. It began to be developed in the first half of 2018 using Node.js and the *framework* for Phaser games. The players control a pirate ship in the ocean, the objective is to survive attacks of other players and for this, it is necessary to collect boxes with ammunition that are in the waters. *multiplayer* is inspired by the Agar.io and Slither.io games, in addition to the most conspicuous games of the *battle royale* genre, such as *Fortnite* and *Playerunknown's Battlegrounds*.

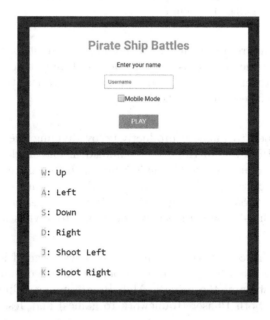

Fig. 4. The initial screen of the game, in this screen the player chooses his nickname to be used to identify before the other players and assignment of his points. It is also necessary to inform if you are going to play on a computer with a keyboard or are using a mobile phone, in which case you have to check the *Mobile Mode* checkbox to set the *joystick* to the touchscreen version *touchscreen*.

Figure 4 shows the initial screen of the game, in this screen the player chooses his nickname to be used to identify to the other players and the attribution of his points. It is also necessary to inform if you are going to play on a computer with a keyboard or are using a mobile phone, in which case you have to check the *Mobile Mode* checkbox to set the *joystick* to the touchscreen version *touchscreen*. This is the Socio-Technical aspect, the game is online, to be played with other people and the technological part is this WebSite of the game that allows to play online with other players and compute their points, visualize the names and points of the opponents to know if is winning or not. Gain is hit or hits an opponent or transposes the circle of death you can see an explosion on the ship representing damage suffered.

The Socio-Technical game reported here in the form of this action research, it was developed during the three cycles described below.

4.2   First Cycle

Plan: Learn how to use an open-source library called Phaser to help with game programming. Because of the online Socio-Technical game on the internet, the team will have to learn how to use the open-source Jest library to be able to do the automated tests in javascript and start programming the tests and some simpler requirements like the login screen.

Act: Split into two groups of Mob Programming. The first focusing on Phaser and the second on the Jest. It is a small Mob with only three people in each group. However, it was chosen to avoid a programmer to lose the concentration if he has not the possession of the keyboard.

Observe: It helped to increase productivity by dividing the group into two groups of three. However, in the end, we unified in one single Mob, everyone around a single computer for share the learning with the entire team.

Figure 5 is a picture of the team using Mob Programming during the development of the *Pirate Ship Battles* game. The pilot in possession of the keyboard types while the others provided ideas, reviewed and told what was to be done.

Reflect: The group cooperatively agreed that it was a good idea to start by learning and doing the tests and also to deepen the knowledge in Phaser should help in the next steps of the project. Mob Programming helped a lot to collaboratively learn both Phaser (framework to games) and Jest (framework to testing).

In the excerpt from the interview where Mob Programming was asked to be useful for this, the answers were unanimous: "Yes". The audio of the interview is available at http://ccsl.ime.usp.br/wiki/MobProgrammingInterviews.

Fig. 5. Mob Programing during the development of the game *Battle Royale* called *Pirate Ship Battles*.

4.3   Second Cycle

Plan: Since the game is of the genre *battle royale* it is necessary to program a circle of death, in which the player suffers damage when crossing that circle. Create a *scoreboard* and minimap.

Act: Split into Mob Programming groups. The first for programming the circle of death and the second creating a scoreboard and minimap. Could use Simultaneous Style Pair Programming to reduce the time-to-benefit.

Observe: Due to the difficulty of programming the circle of death, *Mob Programming* has proved to be a very effective practice here. However, due to pressure of the customer per features with a short deadline. The team decides try the Simultaneous Style Pair Programming in the development of the scoreboard and minimap. Figure 6 shows three players playing a match, each with their computer playing online, each in a different city. They played several games then and we captured the screen to exemplify here. One can see the islands for refueling ammunition, stones that are obstacles to increasing the level of difficulty of the game. There is a minimap in the upper right corner. In the left corner, you can see the *scoreboard*.

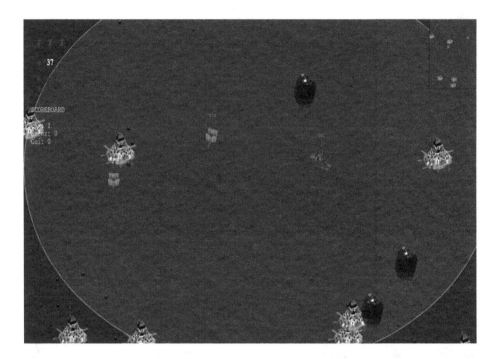

Fig. 6. Three players playing a game. One can see the islands for refueling ammunition, stones that are obstacles to increasing the level of difficulty of the game. There is a minimap in the upper right corner. In the left corner, you can see the *scoreboard*.

Reflect: The group agreed that *Mob Programming* has proved to be a very effective practice in developing the circle of death because of its complexity. In the excerpt from the interview where Mob Programming was asked to be useful for programming complex tasks, the answers were unanimous: "Yes, very useful", "All together gives more confidence", "In the circle of death, there was a union of skills for the task to be done". The audio of the interview is available at http://ccsl.ime.usp.br/wiki/MobProgrammingInterviews.

4.4 Third Cycle

Plan: Program the visual effects of damage both when the ship is shot from an opponent and when the player crosses the circle of death. Create islands for replenishing ammunition and rocks that strike the ship by hitting them.

Act: Split into Mob Programming groups. The first programming the visual effects of damage both when the ship is shot from an opponent and when the player crosses the circle of death. The second by creating islands for the replenishment of ammunition and rocks that hit the ship by hitting them.

Observe: Automated testing has greatly facilitated new implementations of this cycle. Figure 7 shows the explosion, which is the visual damage suffered when a ship transits the circle of death or is hit by an opponent. In the upper right corner, next to the minimap is the explosion, as the ship has broken the circle of death and after a few seconds, it explodes symbolizing damage and loss of life.

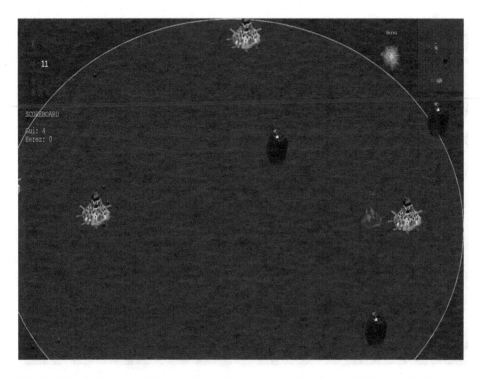

Fig. 7. Visual damage suffered when a ship transits the circle of death or is hit by an opponent. In the upper right corner, next to the minimap is the explosion, as the ship has broken the circle of death and after a few seconds, it explodes symbolizing damage and loss of life.

Reflect: Mob Programming was much more fun in testing compared to testing alone, because when something went wrong running a new code, as everyone was seeing on the projector, it was much more fun to test altogether in the group's opinion as shown in Fig. 5 and in the audio of the interviews made [26].

5   Results Analysis and Discussion

The Socio-Technical game described here is in the form of open science and with its source code also open for audits and collaborations. The source code is on GitHub at: https://github.com/uspgamedev/Pirate-ship-battles.

Figure 8 shows the game working, which is the boat navigating inside the death circle. In the upper right corner is the Minimap. In the left side are the scoreboard and the quantity of ammunition. The stones are to increase the difficulty level, so the player needs to avoid them. The islands are for recovery the ammunition. If a player shoots and it reaches another boat, he/she increases his/her points.

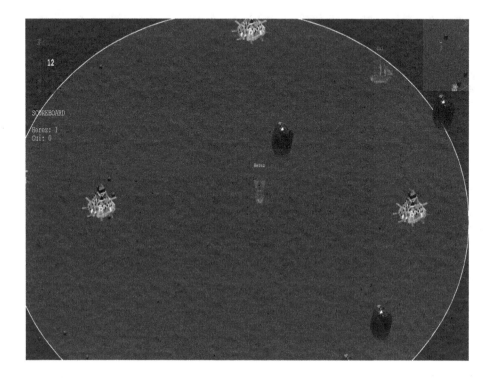

Fig. 8. Game in action.

During the first demonstration of the game running in the classroom on December 5, 2018, a fact occurred characterizing that the way the game was programmed characterizes *Pirate Ship Battles* as a social computing, because it has relation with characteristics of the society in which this game is inserted and being played by humans belonging to that society. The fact happened was related to the Brazilian presidential elections, whose winner is nicknamed Mito by his voters, he is favorable to the population, then one of the students entered the WebSite of the game and logged under the nickname 'Myth' and tried very hard to chase and shoot at all the other players, so the entire Mob had fun laughing at that fact, characterizing this aspect of game programming as social computing.

The result of developing using Mob Programming techniques and Simultaneous Style Pair Programming [22,23] is a system code of excellent quality as shown in Fig. 9.

The CodeClimate shown in Fig. 9 is a free web platform for *open source* projects for collaborative evaluation of its source code. Able to evaluate the source code with the most popular source code management systems (such as Git for example), only providing its address on the internet.

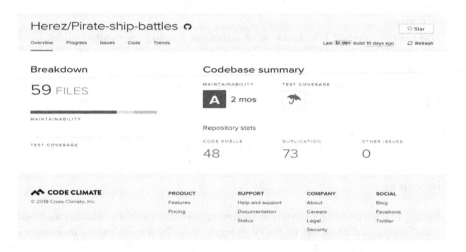

Fig. 9. Source code rated by A at CodeClimate.

6   Limitations

It may be difficult to make generalizations with the discoveries made through action research [13]. I agree with Rose et al. [13] my opinion as a researcher is the fact that the team under research got well together impacted the social aspects studied in this research difficulting the generalizations, e.g., if have another programming task (not as fun as programming a game) would the research results be the same? I consider this one limitation that needs to be more investigated, if the testing activities was funnier here because of the programming task was a game.

Another potential weakness according to Rapoport [27] draws attention to the risk of the researcher becoming overly involved in the situation or of being used as a tool in organizational policy. I think the fact of I was one of the developers and the researcher do not affect in any way the results and there was not any organizational policy involved, it was only a game developed at the university.

7   Conclusion

The action research was adequate for this work, it helped to deepen the knowledge about *Mob Programming* in a structured way by cycles as they appeared the challenges of the development of the game, another positive fact is that the action research done is auditable future, since all interviews, metrics collected, and all game source code is 100% available on the internet.

The team reported was funnier to test altogether, when some mistake happens to run new code, everybody paying attention to the projector on the fault, a ready joke.

The source code of the game is of excellent quality as evaluated by Code-Climate by classifying it with note A, a possible reason for this was during the development to have used the techniques of Mob Programming and Simultaneous Style Pair Programming. The Socio-technical approach proved to be effective in this case of study collaboration techniques in software development.

Acknowledgments. This study was financed in part by the Coordenacao de Aperfeicoamento de Pessoal de Nivel Superior - Brasil (CAPES) - Finance Code 001.

References

1. Eason, K.: Sociotechnical systems theory in the 21st Century: another half-filled glass? Published in Sense in Social Science: A collection of essays in honour of Dr. Lisl Klein edited and published by Desmond Graves, Broughton, pp. 123–134 (2008)
2. Takala, M., Ing, D., Emery, M., Hammond, D., Metcalf, G.: Revisiting the socio-ecological, socio-technical and socio-psychological perspectives. In: 16th International Federation for Systems Research (IFSR) Conversation (2012)
3. Adelman, C.: Kurt Lewin and the origins of action research. Educ. Action Res. **1**(1), 7–24 (1993). https://doi.org/10.1080/0965079930010102
4. Cartwright, D., Zander, A.: Group Dynamics. Tavistock, London (1953)
5. Robertson, D., Giunchiglia, F.: Programming the social computer. Philos. Trans. R. Soc. A **371**, 20120379 (2013). https://doi.org/10.1098/rsta.2012.0379
6. Hohman, M., Slocum, A.: Mob Programming and the Transition to XP. Chigado - IL/USA, Agosto (2001)
7. Zuill, W.: Mob Programming: A Whole Team Approach. Experience report, Agile (2014)
8. Goldman, A., Santos, V.: Continuous Improvement of an XP Laboratory Course: An 18 year History. Experience report, Agile (2019)
9. Zuill, W., Meadows, K.: Mob Programming - A Whole Team Approach. This book is 95% complete (2016). Last updated on 29 Oct 2016
10. Thiollent, M.: Metodologia da pesquisa-ação, 18. edn., 136 p. Cortez, São Paulo (2011)
11. Mumford, E.: The story of socio-technical design: reflections on its successes, failures and potential. Inf. Syst. J. **16**, 317–342 (2006)
12. Kemmis, S., Mctaggart, R., Nixon, R.: The Action Research Planner: Doing Critical Participatory Action Research. Springer, Singapore (2013). https://doi.org/10.1007/978-981-4560-67-2. ISBN 9789814560672

13. Rose, S., Spinks, N., Canhoto, A.I.: Management Research: Applying the Principles. Taylor & Francis (2014). ISBN 9781317819141
14. Coplien, J.O., Harrison, N.B.: Organizational Patterns of Agile Software Development. Prentice-Hall Inc., Upper Saddle River (2004)
15. Pithon, A.J.C.: Projeto organizacional para a engenharia concorrente no ambito das empresas virtuais. Doctoral Thesis. Escola de Engenharia da Universidade do Minho Departamento de Producao e Sistemas, Portugal (2004)
16. Kattan, H.M.: Programming and review simultaneous in Pairs: a pair programming extension. Master dissertation. In: Institute for Technological Research of the Sao Paulo State (2015). https://doi.org/10.13140/RG.2.2.15831.68004
17. Kattan, H.M.: Illuminated arrow: a research method to software engineering based on action research, systematic review and grounded theory. In: CONTECSI 2016, 13th International Conference on Information Systems and Technology Management, pp. 1971–1978 (2016). https://doi.org/10.5748/9788599693124-13CONTECSI/PS-3926. Paper submission: 1 Dec 2015 - Presented at Session4A - AUD Systems Auditing and IT Governance 02/Jun/16-15H30
18. Kattan, H.M.: Those who fail to learn from history are doomed to repeat it. In: Agile Processes in Software Engineering and Extreme Programming: Poster Presented in the 18th International Conference on Agile Software Development, XP 2017. Held in Cologne, Germany, 22–26 May 2017
19. Moise Kattan, H., Goldman, A.: Software development practices patterns. In: Baumeister, H., Lichter, H., Riebisch, M. (eds.) XP 2017. LNBIP, vol. 283, pp. 298–303. Springer, Cham (2017). https://doi.org/10.1007/978-3-319-57633-6_23
20. Kattan, H.M., Oliveira, F., Goldman, A., Yoder, J.W.: Mob programming: the state of the art and three case studies of open source software. In: Santos, V.A., Pinto, G.H.L., Serra Seca Neto, A.G. (eds.) WBMA 2017. CCIS, vol. 802, pp. 146–160. Springer, Cham (2018). https://doi.org/10.1007/978-3-319-73673-0_12
21. Kattan, H.M.: Theory of altruism on software development practices patterns. In: Proceedings of the 19th International Conference on Agile Software Development: Companion (XP 2018), Article 44, 4 pages. ACM, New York (2018). https://doi.org/10.1145/3234152.3314991
22. Kattan, H.M., Soares, F., Goldman, A., Deboni, E., Guerra, E.: Swarm or pair?: strengths and weaknesses of pair programming and mob programming. In: Proceedings of the 19th International Conference on Agile Software Development: Companion (XP 2018), Article 43, 4 pages. ACM, New York (2018). https://doi.org/10.1145/3234152.3234169
23. Kattan, H.M., Soares, F., Goldman, A., Deboni, E., Guerra, E.: Swarm or pair?: strengths and weaknesses of pair programming and mob programming. In: XP 2018, Porto, Portugal, 21–25 May 2018. Poster. https://doi.org/10.13140/RG.2.2.18105.06249
24. Kattan, H.M.: Software development practices patterns: from pair to mob programming. In: Proceedings of the 3th Escola Regional de Engenharia de Software: (ERES 2019). Sociedade Brasileira da Computação (SBC), Rio do Sul, SC, Brazil (2019)
25. Kattan, H.M.: Pair Programming: a step beyond. In: Agile Methods, WBMA 2019. Communications in Computer and Information Science, Springer, Cham (2019)
26. http://ccsl.ime.usp.br/wiki/MobProgrammingInterviews
27. Rapoport, R.N.: Three dilemmas in action research: with special reference to the Tavistock experience. Hum. Relat. **23**(6), 499–513 (1970). https://doi.org/10.1177/001872677002300601

Agile in Education

Mining Undergraduate Students' Code Repositories: Insights from Interdisciplinary Software Projects

Ana Paula dos Santos, Bernardo Baptista, Carlos Felipe Arantes⬤,
Eric Ribeiro, Patrick Rodrigues Galdino, Pedro Pongelupe Lopes,
and Marcelo Werneck Barbosa$^{(\boxtimes)}$⬤

Pontifícia Universidade Católica de Minas Gerais,
Belo Horizonte, Minas Gerais, Brazil
{ana.santos,bernardo.baptista,carlos.arantes,
eric.delgado,patrick.galdino,
pedro.pongelupe}@sga.pucminas.br,
mwerneck@pucminas.br

Abstract. Due to its multidisciplinary and dynamic nature, it is challenging to design Software Engineering (SE) educational material. To do so, universities must consider the complex working environments; recent technologies; and tools and skills, in order to prepare students to fulfill the expectations of the software industry. This study was carried out in a Brazilian private university, specifically in courses called Interdisciplinary Software Project (ISP) of the SE major. These courses are project-based, conducted by two professors at the same time in classroom, following a Scrum-like process. The objective of this study was to characterize how students work and collaborate in a group environment where agile development is used as well as how their behavior reflect on the use of Software Configuration Management (SCM) practices. In order to achieve this objective, the study analyzed 38 students' code repositories. This study has found out that students procrastinate sprint work, since 51% of the commits are performed when less than 20% of the sprint time is left. We have also observed that in 87% of the groups just one member is a top contributor and would harm the projects' outcomes if he/she left the project. In terms of SCM practices, we have identified that most commits comprised changes in up to three files. Moreover, most commit messages are less than 10 words long. This could mean that students do not commit many alterations at the same time but could make better use of messages in order to facilitate the comprehension of alterations by other members.

Keywords: Agile learning · Mining software repositories · Software engineering education

1 Introduction

The requirement for organizations to become more responsive to the needs of customers, the changing conditions of competition and increasing levels of environmental turbulence had driven interest in the concept of agility [1]. Agile is a concept both pertaining

P. Meirelles et al. (Eds.): WBMA 2019, CCIS 1106, pp. 61–75, 2019.
https://doi.org/10.1007/978-3-030-36701-5_5

to organizations as a whole as well as to projects and software development. In software development, agile methods were first introduced by the Agile Manifesto, which values (1) Individuals and interactions over processes and tools; (2) Working software over comprehensive documentation; (3) Customer collaboration over contract negotiation; (4) Responding to change over following a plan [2]. Probably one of the main contributors to the success of agile methods is the dissatisfaction with the bureaucracy of traditional development methodologies since they require less documentation and promote implementation based on informal collaborations between stakeholders [3].

Agile methodologies contrast with traditional project management approaches. Some of their practices include emphasizing continuous design, flexible scope, specifying design features as late as possible, embracing uncertainty and customer interaction, and a self-organized project team organization. Agile is described as iterative and incremental, seeking to avoid the standard approaches that emphasize early design and comprehensive documentation, fixed-scope contracts and low customer interaction [4].

Today, the innovation and quality of the software industry's products and services depend to a great extent on the knowledge, ability and talent applied by software engineers [5]. Software development is generally acknowledged as an intellectually challenging activity that typically requires team members to work collectively in order to create a product or service that may be conceptual, changeable, and intangible [6]. Agile methods introduce substantial improvements to the teamwork within a project. This includes a more efficient distribution of roles and responsibilities, task-based work, workflow visualization, frequent communication between team members and clients, and iterative reviews and improvement processes.

Several agile methods have been proposed with distinct strategies for organizing group work, such as Scrum [7], which is the most popular agile methodology today. It is considered a lightweight project management framework based on the empirical process control model and characterized by frequent iterative and incremental inspection and adaptation [8]. Scrum proposes a rotation of roles, partial deliveries of work in short iterations (sprints), frequent task evaluation, regular meetings, organization of work in task blocks, and shared responsibility between team members [7].

Collaboration and teamwork are as important as the technical skills for the future software engineers, because students will be involved in industrial software projects in which they will need to work in teams [9]. The community of Software Engineering (SE) educators recognizes the importance of preparing SE graduates for the realities of a professional career [10] and many researchers have acknowledged the need to teach agile software development in software engineering programs [11].

Software engineering has a multidisciplinary and dynamic nature that makes it challenging to design its educational material [12]. While developing SE curricula, universities must consider the complex working environments; recent technologies; and tools and skills, in order to prepare their students to fulfill the expectations of the software industry [12]. In order to work well in teams, software developers and SE students need to use Software Configuration Management (SCM) to store, control the version and evolution of different software artifacts, including software code. SCM is a cornerstone subject in SE under graduation courses since it helps to manage the evolution of software artifacts and their documentation. SCM is the discipline for controlling the evolution of complex software systems, helping manage changes to artifacts and ensuring correctness and consistency of systems [13]. Researchers corroborate this idea by stating that there is an insufficient coverage of SCM topics and, although a configuration management course is delivered as an elective in some universities, it should be given as a core course to ensure covering its main areas and practices. Besides, SCM is of high importance in industry [14].

Researchers strongly recommend the development of software projects in teams and the use of collaborative development tools in SE courses for undergraduate students. By doing this, students become more enthusiastic to learn and experience new approaches and tools in software development [9]. Considering this context, this study assesses code repository data in SE undergraduate courses in a private university in Brazil. The objective of such analysis is to characterize how students work and collaborate in a group environment as well as how their behavior reflect on the use of SCM practices. These repositories are created in a course called Interdisciplinary Software Project (ISP). It is a project-based course conducted by two professors at the same time in a classroom. Professors assume the role of supervisors of the project, mentors and facilitators. They have different expertise and are familiar with different areas of the curriculum to provide students with sufficient multidisciplinary guidance for their projects. The classes are fully devoted to building software projects [15].

The remaining sections of this paper are organized as follows. Section 2 presents the Theoretical Background, giving emphasis to teaching agile methods and mining software repositories. Section 3 describes the methodology used in this study. Section 4 presents the results of this work while Sect. 5 presents our conclusions, limitations to this study and suggestions for future work.

2 Theoretical Background

2.1 Agile Learning

Agile learning implies that learners create content and develop skills alongside teachers in a collaborative yet competitive environment. The role of the teacher is centered on facilitation and project direction from an informed perspective. Learners become self-directed, team-oriented, and individually resilient lifelong learners [7]. It has long been acknowledged that learning agile is best done through practical hands-on projects [11] carried out in groups. Teamwork is one of the key competencies that students must acquire to meet the needs and skills of the labor market. The capacity to work in groups is of particular importance, as many jobs are becoming too diverse for just one person to effectively complete [7]. It is, though, necessary to evolve the traditional current education systems which focus and emphasize individual work, while the industrial environment requires cooperative and collaborative work in small to large teams [9].

Due to such changes in education, the Agile Manifesto in Higher Education [16] was developed. It defines four guiding principles for extending the agile principles into the educational context: (a) teachers and students over administration and infrastructure, (b) competence and collaboration over compliance and competition, (c) employability and marketability over syllabus and marks, and (d) attitude and learning skills over aptitude and degree. In brief, the aim of agile learning is to receive continuous feedback, learn from previous iterations and improve on future iterations. Agile learning initiatives should consider those principles.

Although several benefits derive from the adoption of the agile learning methodology, Masood, Hoda and Blincoe [11] identified some constraints students face while applying agile practices in a university course. These constraints include difficulties in setting up common time for all team members to work together, limited availability of customer due to busy schedule and the modifications the students introduced to adapt agile practices to suit the university context, such as daily stand-ups with reduced frequency and combining sprint meetings.

2.2 Mining Software Repositories

With the shift of focus from software product characteristics to more team-based issues, and the increased attention given to people and their work practices during software development, repositories have played an increasingly important role in providing artifacts to enable various explorations [6]. Software projects accumulate a wealth of information over projects' lives, which can shed light on software engineers' coding habits that would cause defects or indicate a developer's special proficiency [17]. Historical and valuable information stored in software repositories provide a great opportunity to acquire knowledge and help in monitoring complex projects and products without interfering with development activities and deadlines [18]. Software repositories such as source control and bug repositories are commonly used to record information about the evolution and progress of the software. The SE community analyzes and explores the rich data available in software repositories to uncover interesting and actionable information about software systems [19]. In particular, repositories have gained prominence as sources of information for those studying team behaviors, enabling researchers to study software practitioners' involvement in detail, and performance in development and maintenance activities [6].

The Mining Software Repositories (MSR) research field, one of the interesting and fastest growing fields within software engineering, focuses on extracting and analyzing the heterogeneous data available in software repositories to uncover interesting, useful, and actionable information about software system and projects. It is aimed to explore the potential of this valuable data in order to better understand and manage projects and also to produce high reliable software system delivered on time and within estimated budget [18]. As so, code repositories contain a wealth of implicit information that can be used to answer many questions about a project's development process, such as who worked on specific files, which developers collaborate, or what is the impact of a change on a specific item.

3 Methodology

3.1 Research Questions and Hypotheses

This study can be characterized as exploratory, since it intends to provide insights into how undergraduate software engineering students have been implementing software and using configuration management tools in agile contexts. In order to better explain how we have analyzed students' behavior, this study's objective was decomposed into research questions, presented as follows.

Procrastination relates to delays that are unjustified, that cannot be defended on grounds of more urgent or important commitments [20]. Procrastination is formally defined as "the voluntary delay of an intended and necessary and/or important activity, despite expecting potential negative consequences that outweigh the positive consequences of the delay" [21]. In an academic environment, higher levels of procrastination in some courses may yield lower grades. University students often have to handle the requirements of multiple courses while also managing several competing activities and responsibilities (inside and outside university). Since time is a limited resource, even students who are not typically considered as procrastinators will sometimes irrationally delay the completion of their schoolwork [22]. Thus, academic procrastination seems to be a risk factor for students' academic performance, physical and mental health, as well as affective and cognitive subjective well-being [23]. In academic agile contexts, since students are not fully allocated to projects, in our understanding, procrastination would be equivalent to not homogeneously using the time devoted to each Sprint, instead, leaving most of the Sprint work to be done closer to its ending. This scenario leads to our first research question:

- RQ1: Do students leave most of the Sprint work to its end?

Github is one of the most popular social network platforms, perhaps due to the features and functionality available on its development management tool Git. Using Git, users can easily search through the massive amounts of code, fork code from other users, and create branches for projects [24]. The research community has started mining data from Github, focusing on various aspects such as its structure and collaboration of social coding, code quality, programming languages used, and the types of software development undertakings [24].

Github repositories can be used to analyze a system's Truck Factor (TF), which is defined as "the number of people on your team that have to be hit by a truck (or quit) before the project is in serious trouble" [25]. Systems with a low truck factor present strong dependencies towards specific personnel, which indicates that the project has few indispensable contributors. If such knowledgeable personnel abandon the project, the system's lifecycle is seriously compromised. Avelino et al. [25] investigated the truck factor of popular Github applications. The authors found that most Github projects have a small truck factor, typically 1 or 2, which means that those projects do not require many knowledgeable developers [24] or are personal projects. In [26], however, in which the 100-top most popular repositories within different programming languages were analyzed, higher values of Truck Factor were found. In an academic context, a project with a lower truck factor may indicate that few students have contributed to its development. This would indicate that tasks were not evenly divided among students and collaboration among team members was not homogeneous. This leads us to our second research question:

- RQ2: Do all students in an agile team equally contribute to code implementation?

During software development process, changes to software artifacts are hosted in control version systems when an action of committing, the action of software developers submitting a software change to a version control system, takes place. These changes can be documented by using commit messages or commit comments. The purpose behind commit messages is to describe the changes and help encoding rationale behind those changes [27]. Commit messages are important because developers use them to review, validate, understand the commits or locate and re(assign) bug reports, and trace changes to other artifacts [27, 28]. Comments convey useful information about the system functionalities and many methods for software engineering tasks take comments as an important source such as code semantic analysis, code reuse and soon. The scope of a comment means a region where the comment refers to in the program. It contains a few statements that match the description or implement the functionality mentioned in the comment [29]. In general, commit messages are an important source of information, knowledge, and documentation that developers rely upon while addressing software maintenance task [27], but commit messages sometimes are non-informative or even empty [28]. In order to facilitate group work and software evolution, in agile educational projects, we expect students to use comments correctly while committing changes. We also expect them to adopt good SCM practices, such as commenting each commit action with useful information as well as not working on too many changes without committing them, which could lead to future conflicts with changes committed by other developers. This leads us to our third research question:

- RQ3: In agile educational projects, how do students use commit comments?

3.2   Interdisciplinary Software Projects

This study was carried out in Interdisciplinary Software Project courses of a Software Engineering major offered by a private Brazilian university. In this major, up to the third year, students have an ISP course each semester whose intention is to serve as a hands-on opportunity to practice what they have learned in the current semester in other courses. In all ISP courses, students work in groups to develop software. ISP III is focused on Requirements Engineering. It introduces the necessity of eliciting and developing requirements with a real client and deliver the implemented software. ISP IV is focused on social projects while ISP V is concerned with software architecture definition and documentation and the software needs to be deployed into mobile devices. From ISP III to ISP V, students need to follow a Scrum-like process. ISP I and II were not included in this study since they are not aimed at implementing complete deliverable software.

The following practices and activities are implemented in these courses:

- Students elicit requirements and document them in user stories format. Students elaborate a Vision document that contains: the problem faced by the client, the general scope of the project, a list of future users and a list of prioritized requirements documented in a user stories format (including non-functional requirements). User stories are estimated with story points. A Product Backlog is created and managed in Trello or a similar tool;
- Work is planned and organized in Sprints. At the first time the courses were provided, the project work was divided into 3 sprints. However, while monitoring

students' work, teachers observed that with longer sprints, students left almost all the work to be done at the end of the sprint. So, projects are currently usually executed in five 15-days development sprints;

- At the beginning of a Sprint, students calculate their velocity and take the top priority stories to be implemented in that Sprint. Tasks are derived from each user story and registered in Trello (Sprint Planning);
- During the Sprint, students need to develop requirements from the prioritized user stories in a use case format (since this is a required competence) and implement software according to the identified tasks;
- At the end of the Sprint, students demonstrate the implemented increment to teachers, who act as user proxies, since the real client is not available to run acceptance tests (Sprint Review);
- At the end of the Sprint, the group needs to reflect on how they have worked as a team. They gather and document lessons learned (Sprint Retrospective);
- Students are assessed according to the software increment delivered, its documentation, whether or not they have gathered lessons learned and how tasks were divided among the team. In case one student does not participate in software implementation, his/her grade is reduced.

In order to perform this study, students were asked to provide a link to their code repositories. Data was obtained from those repositories and was transferred to a database, which contains the information needed to perform this study. This is in compliance with [30], who said that own datasets are used in half of the papers reviewed instead of publicly accessible datasets.

Table 1 shows the number of repositories analyzed according to the semester each course was taken.

Table 1. Number of repositories analyzed.

	2017/01	2017/02	2018/01	2018/02	2019/01	Total
ISP III	1	3	5	0	4	13
ISP IV	0	6	4	4	1	15
ISP V	0	0	1	6	3	10
Total	1	9	10	10	8	38

4 Results and Discussions

This section presents and discusses the results obtained with the analyses of the code repositories. Results are presented according to each research question described previously.

4.1 Procrastination

The first research question (RQ1) was related to student procrastination. The study aims at identifying whether students leave most of the Sprint work to its end. In order to answer this question, since sprints have different durations in all three ISP courses, we calculated for each commit, the percentage of sprint time left to the sprint ending. As so, when a commit is performed on the same day as the sprint starts, the percentage of time left equals 100%. Figure 1 shows the number of commits performed versus the percentage of time remaining for the end of the corresponding sprint. As it can be observed, the majority of commits (around 51% - 934 out of 1805) are performed when less than 20% of the time is left. This corroborates the existence of procrastination among students and that students do not equally distribute their work effort throughout the sprint.

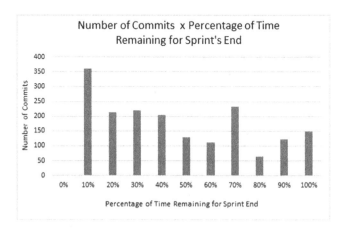

Fig. 1. Procrastination. Number of commits and percentage of time remaining to sprint end.

In agile projects, where the development team is completely allocated to one project, the team is fully dedicated to implement the project's tasks. However, in an academic project, students are not fully allocated to just one project or assignment. Anyway, it is expected that they make good use of their time to carry out as many tasks and deliver as many requirements as they can. Since agile projects do not work with a fixed scope, requirements are implemented according to the team's velocity as well as to the requirements' priorities. If students did not procrastinate much, more requirements could be delivered and, in terms of students' learning process, they might have more opportunities to put into practice what they have learned.

4.2   Team Work and Collaboration

The second research question (RQ2) was related to student teamwork and collaboration. The study aims at identifying whether students in a team equally contribute to code implementation. In order to answer this question, we have calculated the truck factor for each project, as suggested in [25]. Table 2 shows the number of projects, for each type of IPS course, distributed according to the calculated Truck Factor.

Table 2. Number of projects according to their Truck Factor.

	TF = 1	TF = 2	TF = 3	TF = 4	TF = 5
ISP III	10	3	0	0	0
ISP IV	13	2	0	0	0
ISP V	7	3	0	0	0
Total	30	8	0	0	0

As it can be observed, most of the projects have a Truck Factor equal to 1. This means that in most groups just one member is essential to the outcomes of the project. In an agile educational context, this could mean that one student is assuming most of the development work or even that students are not equally distributing the projects' tasks among them. This result may be analyzed coupled with the result obtained in terms of procrastination. The higher number of commits performed closer to the end of the sprint might indicate that most members are working just on the last days of the sprint, leaving the work at its beginning to just one or two members. This result indicates that teachers should pay even more attention to students' participation and that students should be taught how to manage and distribute their tasks.

Since ISP projects can have different numbers of members, we have also calculated the percentage of members that were classified as top contributors, according to the Truck Factor algorithm. Figure 2 shows this distribution. In more than 76% of the projects, less than 40% of the team (by summing the number of repositories in the first two columns) were identified as top contributors according to the algorithm. Teams are composed from 2 to 5 members.

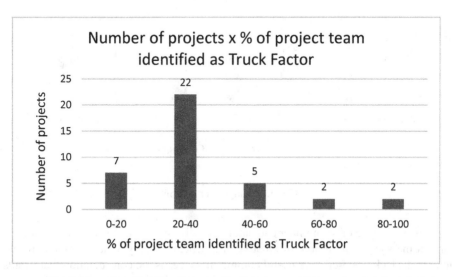

Fig. 2. Percentage of members classified as top contributors (truck factor).

4.3   Commit Messages

The third research question (RQ3) was related to the use of good SCM practices, especially those corresponding to committing files. The study aims at identifying whether students take longer to perform a commit, leaving a great amount of work to be committed at the same time, which could increase the probability of conflicts. Besides, agile projects are grounded on practices such as continuous delivery and integration and automated testing that demand the repository code be constantly checked. In order to answer this question, we have analyzed the number of files committed at the same time as well as the content of each commit comment.

There is no standard definition of what a commit granularity of a change is, or whether it is too small or too large. Researchers usually classify changes into 3 categories: number of modified, added, and removed files [31]. In order to assess whether or not students commit many changes at the same time, we have counted the number of changes (file insertions, alterations and deletions) performed together with each commit. It is possible to observe that students have followed the guideline of committing few files at the same time, not performing many alterations that would be committed at the same time, increasing the chances of conflicts. Out of the 2,414 commits analyzed, 55.17% have included changes in up to three files. On the other hand, only 54 have changed more than 100 files and only 15 of these 54 commits have changed more than 1,000 files. A closer look at these commits revealed that they comprised the inclusion or deletion of complete component libraries (Fig. 3).

Fig. 3. Changes per commit

Mostly because of the number and nature of daily activities by software developers, commit messages can be non-informative or practically empty. One possible explanation for the lack of descriptive/useful commit messages is the consideration that details about the changes and changed code units generated with line-based differencing tools are enough for understanding the change [27]. In order to assess if students are writing useful commit messages, we have counted the words in each commit. Figure 4 shows the distribution of comments' length. We can see that most commit messages are less than 10 words long. This results is in accordance with [31], who found out in a similar study that the median number of words in commit messages ranged from 4 to 10 depending on the project, and in all projects the commit messages were less than 25 words at least 75% of the time.

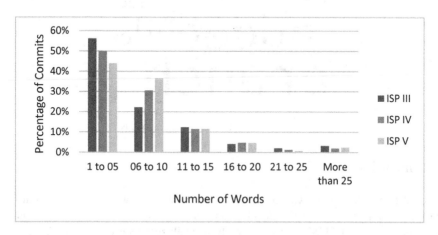

Fig. 4. Comments' length

Since agile projects are not based on comprehensive documentation and, usually, other different types of documentation are demanded, being clear and complete in commit messages could help build a set of information that might be retrieved in case of need or when an evolution is planned.

In an attempt to automatically generate commit messages, the study [28] found out that nearly half of the commit messages begin with a verb followed by a direct object. Authors observed that most used verbs are: add, create, make, implement, fix, remove, update, upgrade, use, move, change. Figure 5 shows a word cloud with the top 25 words obtained from commit messages in our study. Our findings corroborate those of [28] since the words used most frequently are verbs that reflect the actions developers take: merging, adding, creating, among others.

Fig. 5. Word cloud for commit comments

5   Conclusions

The objective of this study was to characterize how students work and collaborate in a group environment where agile development is used as well as how their behavior reflect on the use of SCM practices. We have analyzed code repositories created in Interdisciplinary Software Project (ISP) courses, project-based courses conducted by two or three professors at the same time in a classroom with the objective of producing software in an agile way. More specifically, this study aimed at assessing whether or not students procrastinate their work, which in an agile context means that they do not equally distribute their effort throughout iterations. Moreover, we have analyzed whether few students assume most of the work to be done and the use of some SCM practices, which also could impact team performance in agile projects.

This study has found out that students do really procrastinate sprint work, since the majority of commits (around 51%) are performed when less than 20% of the sprint time is left. We have also observed that most students' projects presented a Truck Factor equal to 1. This means that in most groups (86.84%) just one member is a top contributor and would harm the projects' outcomes if the/she left the project. In other words, just one or two students are assuming most of the development work or even that some students have a poor contribution to projects' success. The analyses of commit messages revealed that most commits comprised changes in up to three files. Moreover, most commit messages are less than 10 words long. This could mean that students do not commit many alterations at the same time but could make better use of commit messages in order to facilitate the comprehension of alterations by other members.

5.1 Limitations and Threats to Validity

As limitations to this study, we could highlight that this study analyzes only code repositories in one Software Engineering major in Brazil. Comparing these results with ones obtained in different courses or majors could shed light into differences among countries or student profiles. Besides, we have only relied on information persisted in code repositories. The use of qualitative methods such as interviews or focus groups could be used to better comprehend and validate the information obtained through this study, which could lead to different or additional results.

Besides, we could only rely on information already available in code repositories. For instance, we have not considered the work-in-progress (WIP) and size of the tasks/stories (estimations), since this information was not available in such repositories. Although developers are oriented to continually commit their work to avoid conflicts, due to the absence of information on stories size, we cannot affirm whether commits appearing closer to the end of the sprint are due to procrastination or just opportunity or efficiency.

5.2 Contributions and Future Work

This study has some contributions. To agile practitioners, this study shows that agile teachers or instructors should emphasize some agile practices in their courses. Procrastination is not an attitude that should be avoided in agile teams. Agile team members should use their time as best as they can and should be focused on software development and delivery all the time. Besides, team members should be more worried on better distributing tasks among team members. In fact, students should display a more proactive attitude towards identifying the undone tasks that could be done by them.

This work opens up some opportunities for future work. The study has identified some improvements for agile teachers that could be implemented in these ISP courses. Besides, assessing how specific students evolve and perform from ISP III course to ISP V could lead to interesting results. Above all, it should be highlighted that ISP courses are a great opportunity for students to learn not only about software development but also to develop soft skills related to teamwork, collaboration and negotiation. Previous research [11] has identified some constraints students face while applying agile practices in university courses such as difficulties in setting up common time for everyone to work together, customer availability and adaptation of agile practices. Besides, this study stimulates professors to try and avoid the pitfalls of letting students, working in part-time projects, to be really agile, and benefit from it, since they are not always co-located (in space and time), and not focused only in a single project or assignment. For instance, professors should stimulate the use of alternative communication tools (e.g. virtual daily meetings software). Taking this into account, we are aware that improving ISP courses considering the outcomes of this study will lead to an even more enriching experience to students.

References

1. Power, D.J., Sohal, A.S., Rahman, S.-U.: Critical success factors in agile supply chain management - an empirical study. Int. J. Phys. **31**, 247–265 (2001)
2. Beck, K., et al.: Manifesto for agile software development. Agil. Alliance **2009**, 2006 (2001)
3. Rubin, E., Rubin, H.: Supporting agile software development through active documentation. Requir. Eng. **16**, 117–132 (2011). https://doi.org/10.1007/s00766-010-0113-9
4. Serrador, P., Pinto, J.K.: Does Agile work? - a quantitative analysis of agile project success. Int. J. Proj. Manag. **33**, 1040–1051 (2015). https://doi.org/10.1016/j.ijproman.2015.01.006
5. Colomo-palacios, R., Casado-lumbreras, C., Soto-acosta, P., García-peñalvo, F.J., Tovar-caro, E.: Competence gaps in software personnel: a multi-organizational study. Comput. Hum. Behav. **29**, 456–461 (2013). https://doi.org/10.1016/j.chb.2012.04.021
6. Licorish, S.A., Macdonell, S.G.: Exploring software developers' work practices: task differences, participation, engagement, and speed of task resolution. Inf. Manag. **54**, 364–382 (2017). https://doi.org/10.1016/j.im.2016.09.005
7. Noguera, I., Guerrero-rold, A., Masó, R.: Collaborative agile learning in online environments: strategies for improving team regulation and project management. Comput. Educ. **116**, 110–129 (2018). https://doi.org/10.1016/j.compedu.2017.09.008
8. Cubric, M.: An agile method for teaching agile in business schools. Int. J. Manag. Educ. **11**, 119–131 (2013). https://doi.org/10.1016/j.ijme.2013.10.001
9. Raibulet, C., Fontana, F.A.: Collaborative and teamwork software development in an undergraduate software engineering course. J. Syst. Softw. **144**, 409–422 (2018). https://doi.org/10.1016/j.jss.2018.07.010
10. Fornaro, R.J., Heil, M.R., Tharp, A.L.: Reflections on 10 years of sponsored senior design projects: Students win - clients win! J. Syst. Inf. Technol. **80**, 1209–1216 (2007). https://doi.org/10.1016/j.jss.2006.09.052
11. Masood, Z., Hoda, R., Blincoe, K.: Adapting agile practices in university contexts. J. Syst. Softw. **144**, 501–510 (2018). https://doi.org/10.1016/j.jss.2018.07.011
12. Alarifi, A., Zarour, M., Alomar, N., Alshaikh, Z.: SECDEP: software engineering curricula development and evaluation process using SWEBOK. Inf. Softw. Technol. **74**, 114–126 (2016). https://doi.org/10.1016/j.infsof.2016.01.013
13. Mohan, K., Xu, P., Cao, L., Ramesh, B.: Improving change management in software development: integrating traceability and software configuration management. Decis. Support Syst. **45**, 922–936 (2008). https://doi.org/10.1016/j.dss.2008.03.003
14. Moreno, A.M., Sanchez-segura, M., Medina-dominguez, F., Carvajal, L.: Balancing software engineering education and industrial needs. J. Syst. Softw. **85**, 1607–1620 (2012). https://doi.org/10.1016/j.jss.2012.01.060
15. Nelson, M.A.V., Carneiro, R.V., Costa, M.R.: Interdisciplinary software projects as an active methodology to practice for the profession. In: 2017 IEEE/ACM 1st International Workshop on Software Engineering Curricula for Millennials, pp. 28–32. IEEE, Buenos Aires (2017). https://doi.org/10.1109/secm.2017.8
16. Kamat, V.: Agile manifesto in higher education. In: 2012 IEEE Fourth International Conference on Technology for Education, pp. 231–232. IEEE (2012). https://doi.org/10.1109/t4e.2012.49
17. Olatunji, S.O., Idrees, S.U., Al-ghamdi, Y.S., Al-ghamdi, J.S.A.: Mining software repositories – a comparative analysis. Int. J. Comput. Sci. Netw. Secur. **10**, 161–174 (2014)

18. Siddiqui, T., Ahmad, A.: Data mining tools and techniques for mining software repositories: a systematic review. In: Aggarwal, V.B., Bhatnagar, V., Mishra, D.K. (eds.) Big Data Analytics. AISC, vol. 654, pp. 717–726. Springer, Singapore (2018). https://doi.org/10.1007/978-981-10-6620-7_70

19. Sun, X., Li, B., Leung, H., Li, B., Li, Y.: MSR4SM: using topic models to effectively mining software repositories for software maintenance tasks. Inf. Softw. Technol. **66**, 1–12 (2015). https://doi.org/10.1016/j.infsof.2015.05.003

20. Wessel, J., Bradley, G.L., Hood, M.: Comparing effects of active and passive procrastination: a field study of behavioral delay. Pers. Individ. Dif. **139**, 152–157 (2019). https://doi.org/10.1016/j.paid.2018.11.020

21. Grund, A., Fries, S.: Understanding procrastination: a motivational approach. Pers. Individ. Dif. **121**, 120–130 (2018). https://doi.org/10.1016/j.paid.2017.09.035

22. Kljajic, K., Gaudreau, P.: Does it matter if students procrastinate more in some courses than in others? A multilevel perspective on procrastination and academic achievement. Learn. Instr. **58**, 193–200 (2018). https://doi.org/10.1016/j.learninstruc.2018.06.005

23. Grunschel, C., Schwinger, M., Steinmayr, R., Fries, S.: Effects of using motivational regulation strategies on students' academic procrastination, academic performance, and well-being. Learn. Individ. Differ. **49**, 162–170 (2016). https://doi.org/10.1016/j.lindif.2016.06.008

24. Hu, Y., Wang, S., Ren, Y., Choo, K.R.: User influence analysis for Github developer social networks. Expert Syst. Appl. **108**, 108–118 (2018). https://doi.org/10.1016/j.eswa.2018.05.002

25. Ferreira, M., Ferreira, K., Valente, M.T.: A comparison of three algorithms for computing truck factors. In: IEEE International Conference on Program Comprehension (2017)

26. Ferreira, J.J.M., Fernandes, C.I., Ratten, V.: A co-citation bibliometric analysis of strategic management research. Scientometrics **109**, 1–32 (2016). https://doi.org/10.1007/s11192-016-2008-0

27. Linares-vásquez, M., Cortés-coy, L.F., Aponte, J., Poshyvanyk, D., College, T.: ChangeScribe : a tool for automatically generating commit messages. In: IEEE/ACM 37th IEEE International Conference on Software Engineering, Florence, pp. 709–712 (2015) https://doi.org/10.1109/icse.2015.229

28. Jiang, S., Mcmillan, C.: Towards automatic generation of short summaries of commits. In: 2017 IEEE/ACM 25th International Conference on Program Comprehension, pp. 320–323. IEEE (2017). https://doi.org/10.1109/icpc.2017.12

29. Chen, H., Huang, Y., Liu, Z., Chen, X., Zhou, F., Luo, X.: Automatically detecting the scopes of source code comments. J. Syst. Softw. **153**, 45–63 (2019). https://doi.org/10.1016/j.jss.2019.03.010

30. Vandecruys, O., Martens, D., Baesens, B., Mues, C., De Backer, M., Haesen, R.: Mining software repositories for comprehensible software fault prediction models **81**, 823–839 (2008). https://doi.org/10.1016/j.jss.2007.07.034

31. Casalnuovo, C.: Toward generating commit messages for software repositories, University of Delaware (2013)

Initial Assessment of Agile Development in the Undergraduate Curricula

Nicolas Paez[(⊠)] , Alejandro Oliveros , and Diego Fontdevila

Universidad Nacional de Tres de Febrero, Caseros, Argentina
nicopaez@computer.org
{aoliveros,dfontdevila}@untref.edu.ar

Abstract. Agile is the most popular approach for software development nowadays, present in many companies and also in academia. Many universities have included agile in their curricula but there are no formal studies focused in the Argentinean Universities. In this study we aim to make an initial assessment of the state of Agile Education in the context of the Information Technology and Computer Science programs in Argentina. With this goal we conducted a survey in a national conference of Systems Engineering. Our results confirm that Agile is present in the curricula but in most cases it is only covered from a theoretical point of view. We also identified some situations that suggest a lack of depth in the way some practices are taught.

Keywords: Agile · Software Engineering · Education

1 Introduction

Agile Software Development has been growing constantly since the publication of the Agile Manifesto in 2001. The software industry has globally embraced Agile [1] and many universities around the world have included Agile-related topics in the Information Systems and Computer Science programs [2–4]. Even more, some studies have reported very positive results using Agile in capstone courses [5,6]. Classical textbooks on Software Engineering like the works of Pressman and Sommerville have included Agile topics for several editions. ACM has also included Agile in its curricular recommendations for Software Engineering and Information Technology [7]. In Argentina many software companies have adopted Agile methods too [8] and practitioners have generated different community spaces to learn and share experiences using agile [9,10]. Even though some professors have reported experiences with good results teaching Agile in their courses [11,12], the regulations and guidance for the accreditation of Information Technology and Computer Science programs do not mention Agile methods at all [13]. At the time of this writing, there are no formal studies of the current situation of Agile Education in Argentina and this is the motivation for our study. The research questions that guide our work are:

© Springer Nature Switzerland AG 2019
P. Meirelles et al. (Eds.): WBMA 2019, CCIS 1106, pp. 76–84, 2019.
https://doi.org/10.1007/978-3-030-36701-5_6

- Q1: Are Agile methods part of the Information Technology and Computer Science programs in Argentina?
- Q2: Which are the most common agile practices taught in Information Technology and Computer Science programs?

The rest of this article is organized as follows: Sect. 2 reviews related work, Sect. 3 describes the study and the methodology used, Sect. 4 presents the results and relevant findings, Sect. 5 lists the threats to validity and finally Sect. 6 presents our conclusions and future lines of work.

2   Related Work

The search for agile and education produced results from two very different related topics. One is teaching agile software development, the other one is using agile principles and techniques as a teaching approach, independent of the subject matter. This study is focused on the first topic, that is: teaching agile software development.

There are several studies around the world about teaching agile software development. Paasivaara et al. [14] reported an experience using Lego blocks to teach Scrum in Finland. Von Wangenheim et al. [15] developed an educational game called Scrumia for teaching Scrum in computing courses in Brazil. Persson et al. [16] proposed an adaptation of the Scrum framework to suit the particular needs of the learning context of university courses in Sweden. Kropp and Meier [17] described some interesting findings in their research on teaching agile in Switzerland. They highlight the importance of integrating agile software development not only theoretically but also putting it into practice, and they make a proposal for this based on their experience. There are also several reports on the use of agile methods in capstone projects [4–6].

Beyond experience reports, there are some studies reporting evolution and/or state of the art in particular regions which is somewhat similar to our goal. A similar study to ours was carried out in Thailand by Chookittikul et al. [3]. The researchers performed interviews in several leading universities in Thailand to understand how agile methods were incorporated into computer science curricula. A broad study on Agile evolution in Brazil was conducted by Melo et al. [18] which covered industry, education and research but this study did not cover usage of specific practices.

In our search we did not find any study in Argentina focused on understanding the incorporation of agile development education in Universities. We did find some articles reporting experiences of teaching agile. Uva et al. [19] have developed a proposal for documenting capstone projects developed with Agile processes. Levy et al. [20] have reported the use of Scrum for developing software projects in a Software Engineering course at UNLP. Scott et al. [12] have reported several experiences teaching Scrum in Software Engineering courses at UNICEN. We published our own experience teaching Agile Practices using a flipped classroom approach at UNTREF [11].

3   Methodology and Study Description

To perform this initial assessment, we conducted a survey among the participants of the 6th National Congress of Informatics Engineering and Information Systems (CoNaIISI 2018) [21]. This congress is annually organized by RIISIC [22] (Red de Carreras de Ingeniería en Informática/Sistemas de Información del CONFEDI). The 6th edition was on November 2018 and it was hosted at Universidad CAECE in Mar del Plata City. The congress had almost 500 participants. The questionnaire used was structured in the following way:

- The first part included demographic questions about: academic institution, percentage of approved courses and professional experience.
- The second part contained the questions about methodologies, in which the participants were asked to mark the methodologies they had studied.
- The third part had a double-entry matrix question where participants were asked to mark how deeply they had studied a set of agile practices. The possible answers were: (a) Did not study it at the university, (b) I studied it at the university but only from a conceptual viewpoint and (c) I studied it at the university and did some practice.

To select the practices to include in our study we considered the set of practices defined in our umbrella project, previously published in [23]. The resulting set of practices to study is: Automated Tests, Continuous Delivery, Continuous Integration, Iterative Development, Test-Driven Development, Pair-Programming and Retrospectives.

To host the survey, we used Google Forms, an online tool that supports the edition and publication of online forms. It also provides some reports and the possibility of exporting results to a spreadsheet. Using this tool, we did the following:

1. We created the survey questionnaire in Google Forms.
2. We printed several copies of the survey questionnaire.
3. We attended the conference with the copies of the survey questionnaire in paper and with an iPad. This way we gave the respondents the chance to fill the survey online or in paper.
4. We personally instructed each respondent before they started filling the survey and we asked them to answer exclusively considering what they had studied at the university.

4   Results and Findings

We collected 62 data points from 14 different institutions[1]. Most of the participants (68%) responded they had taken more than 50% of the courses of their

---

[1] The whole list of institutions is available at https://doi.org/10.6084/m9.figshare.9730328.

programs (we considered these students and graduates as advanced students). Figure 1 shows the details of the distribution of percentage of student progress based on the number of courses.

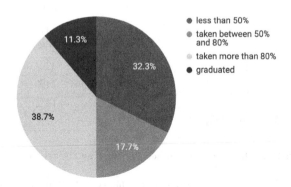

Fig. 1. Percentage of student progress in terms of courses

Regarding professional work experience, more than 50% of the participants indicated some experience. Figure 2 shows the distribution of their work experience.

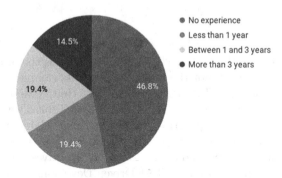

Fig. 2. Work experience

Since Software Engineering courses covering methodology topics are usually located in the second half of the programs we considered appropriate to simultaneously analyze: (a) the whole sample and (b) only advanced students (respondents that have completed at least 50% of the courses in their program). Table 1 shows the results for the question about software development methods studied, detailing results for the whole sample and the advanced students. This was a multiple-choice question where we asked participants to select all the items they studied at the university.

Table 1. Software development methods.

Development methods	Whole sample	Advanced students
Agile methods (in an abstract sense)	68%	76%
Structured Analysis and Design	61%	62%
Scrum	55%	64%
Unified Process	44%	60%
Extreme Programming	31%	43%
DevOps	11%	14%
Kanban	10%	14%
None of the listed methods	13%	7%

Table 2. Agile Practices studied considering the whole sample.

Practice	Not studied	Theory only	Theory and practice
Automated Tests	31%	37%	32%
Continuous Delivery	76%	13%	11%
Continuous Integration	50%	37%	13%
Iterative Development	19%	31%	50%
Test-Driven Development	63%	26%	11%
Pair-Programming	45%	19%	35%
Retrospectives	77%	11%	11%

Table 2 shows the results for the whole sample regarding the practices studied. Table 3 shows the results for the advanced students sample.

The differences between Tables 2 and 3 suggest that Agile is being covered mainly in the second part of the programs. Looking at Table 3 we see that Retrospectives are the least studied practice, even less than Test-Driven Development. This situation is very curious because it is just the opposite of what has been reported by several industry studies [23–25]: Retrospectives are usually among the most widely used practices while Test-Driven Development is usually among the least used practices.

When crossing the answers about software development methods with the answers about software development practices we see two interesting findings:

- 65% of the participants reporting that they studied Scrum state they did not study Retrospectives, which is a key practice of Scrum.
- Along the same line of reasoning we see that 58% of those that responded they studied Extreme Programming state they did not study Test-Driven Development, which is a core practice of Extreme Programming.

Table 3. Agile practices studied considering advance students only.

Practice	Not studied	Theory only	Theory and practice
Iterative development	7%	31%	62%
Test automation	12%	45%	43%
Pair Programming	31%	21%	48%
Continuous Integration	38%	43%	19%
Test-Driven Development	52%	33%	14%
Infra as code	64%	21%	14%
Continuous Delivery	67%	17%	17%
Retrospective	69%	14%	17%

These findings open an interesting question regarding how Agile is been taught in academia, it might be that many of these methods are only being taught superficially, or that specific practices are being excluded. It might also be that the practices have been taught but were not retained by the students.

We also noticed that most respondents who reported to have studied agile practices are also working in the industry. That is 68% of the whole sample answered that they studied agile and 60% of that group has working experience. This suggest an strong relationship between knowledge of agile methods and working at industry. But it may be that the relationship is actually between years of study and working at industry, and the previously described relationship is just a consequence of this one.

5   Threats to Validity

The threats to validity are presented following the categorization provided by Wholin et al. [26]. We found threats in the following two categories:

- Internal: even when we explicitly asked respondents what they studied at the university, it is possible that students answered based on what they learned at work.
- External: the sample used in the study is based on answers from people belonging to only 14 institutions and some important institutions were not part of this sample.

6   Conclusions and Future Work

Our results show that Agile methods and practices are present in the Information Technology and Computer Science programs, 76% of advanced students reported having studied agile methods. This answers our first research question.

Regarding our second research question, four practices are the most studied by advanced students (each one individually exceeds 60%): Continuous Integration, Pair-Programming, Test Automation and Iterative Development.

Beyond our research questions we offer some additional findings. When analyzing concrete Agile practices, we observe that some of them are covered mainly from a theoretical perspective without practical activities.

We also noticed that even when certain methods we reported as studied, some associated key practices were not. This is the case of students reporting to have studied Scrum but not Retrospectives and students reporting to have studied Extreme Programming but not Test-Driven Development.

Some interesting issues were detected regarding the popularity of practices in industry vs their presence in university education: while Retrospectives are one of the most popular agile practices in the industry it is the least studied practice in the university. Another example of this apparent issue is Test Driven Development: it is one of the least used practices in the industry (though very popular) but it is not among the least studied practices. These findings may suggest that industry and academia have different perceptions regarding the relevance of these practices or that the challenges of adoption are not aligned with the challenges of theoretical teaching (i.e. teaching about a practice is not the same as teaching how to perform it).

In order to have a deeper insight on the state of agile education in the Information Technology and Computer Science programs further studies should be conducted to gather information in two dimensions: (1) Study the topic from the perspective of professors and institutions, (2) Study a broader set of practices. These topics will be the focus of the future phase of our research project.

References

1. West, D., Grant, T.: Agile development: mainstream adoption has changed agility. Forrester Res. **2**, 41 (2010)
2. Rodriguez, M.C., Vazquez, M.M., Tslapatas, H., De Carvalho, C.V., Jesmin, T., Heidmann, O.: Introducing lean and agile methodologies into engineering higher education: the cases of Greece, Portugal, Spain and Estonia. Paper presented at the IEEE Global Engineering Education Conference, EDUCON, pp. 720–729, April 2018. https://doi.org/10.1109/EDUCON.2018.8363302
3. Chookittikul, W., Maher, P.E., Kourik, J.L.: Agile methods in Thai higher education and beyond. Paper presented at the 2011 24th IEEE-CS Conference on Software Engineering Education and Training, CSEE and T 2011 - Proceedings, p. 557. https://doi.org/10.1109/CSEET.2011.5876153
4. Rico, D.F., Sayani, H.H.: Use of agile methods in software engineering education. Paper presented at the Proceedings - 2009 Agile Conference, AGILE 2009, pp. 174–179. https://doi.org/10.1109/AGILE.2009.13
5. Mahnic, V.: A capstone course on agile software development using scrum. IEEE Trans. Educ. **55**(1), 99–106 (2012). https://doi.org/10.1109/TE.2011.2142311
6. Lu, B., Declue, T.: Teaching agile methodology in a software engineering capstone course. J. Comput. Sci. Coll. **26**, 293–299 (2011)
7. ACM Curricula Recommendations. https://www.acm.org/education/curricula-recommendations. Accessed 15 July 2019

8. Paez, N., Fontdevila, D., Oliveros, A.: HELENA study: initial observations of software development practices in Argentina. In: Felderer, M., Méndez Fernández, D., Turhan, B., Kalinowski, M., Sarro, F., Winkler, D. (eds.) PROFES 2017. LNCS, vol. 10611, pp. 443–449. Springer, Cham (2017). https://doi.org/10.1007/978-3-319-69926-4_34

9. Meetup Agiles Argentina. https://www.meetup.com/agiles-arg/. Accessed 15 July 2019

10. Agiles Argentina Community Page. http://www.agiles.org/argentina. Accessed 15 July 2019

11. Paez, N.: A flipped classroom experience teaching software engineering. In: IEEE/ACM 1st International Workshop on Software Engineering Curricula for Millennials (SECM), Buenos Aires, pp. 16–20 (2017). https://doi.org/10.1109/SECM.2017.6

12. Scott, W., Rodríguez, G., Soria, A., Campo, M.: Experiences in software engineering education: using scrum, agile coaching, and virtual reality. https://doi.org/10.4018/978-1-5225-3923-0.ch050

13. Ministerio de Educación, "Resolución 786/2009," InfoLEG Información Legislativa. http://servicios.infoleg.gob.ar/infolegInternet/verNorma.do?id=154121. Accessed 15 July 2019

14. Paasivaara, M., Heikkilä, V., Lassenius, C., Toivola, T.: Teaching students scrum using LEGO blocks. In: 36th International Conference on Software Engineering, ICSE Companion 2014 - Proceedings. https://doi.org/10.1145/2591062.2591169

15. Gresse von Wangenheim, C., Savi, R., Borgatto, A.: SCRUMIA–an educational game for teaching SCRUM in computing courses. J. Syst. Softw. **86**, 2675–2687. https://doi.org/10.1016/j.jss.2013.05.030

16. Persson, M., Kruzela, I., Allder, K., Johansson, O., Johansson, P.: On the Use of Scrum in Project Driven Higher Education

17. Kropp, M., Meier, A.: Teaching agile software development at university level: values, management, and craftsmanship. In: 26th International Conference on Software Engineering Education and Training (CSEE&T), San Francisco, CA, pp. 179–188 (2013). https://doi.org/10.1109/CSEET.2013.6595249

18. Melo, O., Santos, C.V., Katayama, E.: The evolution of agile software development in Brazil. J. Braz. Comput. Soc. **19**, 523–552 (2013)

19. Uva, M., Daniele, M., Zorzán, F., Frutos, M., Arsaute, A.: Propuesta para documentar trabajos finales utilizando metodologías ágiles. In: IX Congreso sobre Tecnología en Educación & Educación en Tecnología. La Rioja, Argentina (2014)

20. Levy, S., Romero Dapozo, J., Pasini, A.: Implementación práctica del agilismo en proyecto de Ingeniería de Software. In: XIX Concurso de Trabajos Estudiantiles (EST 2016). Tres de Febrero, Argentina (2016)

21. Congreso Nacional de Ingenieria Informática y Sistemas de Información (2018). https://www.conaiisi2018mdp.org/. Accessed 15 July 2019

22. Red de Ingenieria Informática y Sistemas de Información del Confedi. https://confedi.org.ar/riisic/. Accessed 15 July 2019

23. Paez, N., Fontdevila, D., Oliveros, A.: Characterizing technical and organizational practices in the Agile Community. In: Proceedings of CONAIISI, Salta, Argentina (2016)

24. Paez, N., Fontdevila, D., Gainey, F., Oliveros, A.: Technical and organizational agile practices: a Latin-American survey. In: Garbajosa, J., Wang, X., Aguiar, A. (eds.) XP 2018. LNBIP, vol. 314, pp. 146–159. Springer, Cham (2018). https://doi.org/10.1007/978-3-319-91602-6_10

25. 13th Annual State of Agile Report. Version One (2019). https://www.stateofagile.com/ufh-i-521251909-13th-annual-state-of-agile-report. Accessed 15 July 2019
26. Wohlin, C., Runeson, P., Höst, M., Ohlsson, M.C., Regnell, B., Wesslén, A.: Experimentation in Software Engineering. Springer, Heidelberg (2012). https://doi.org/10.1007/978-3-642-29044-2

Lessons Learned from the Agile Transformation of an Aeronautics Computing Center

Fernando Rodrigues de Sá[1,2]([✉])[iD], Ricardo Godoi Vieira[1][iD],
and Adilson Marques da Cunha[1][iD]

[1] Instituto Tecnológico de Aeronáutica, Praça Marechal do Ar Eduardo Gomes,
no. 50 - Vila das Acácias, São José dos Campos, SP 12228-901, Brazil
{desa,cunha}@ita.br, desafrs@fab.mil.br, rikas.rgv@gmail.com
[2] Centro de Computação da Aeronáutica de São José dos Campos,
Praça Marechal do Ar Eduardo Gomes, no. 50 - Vila das Acácias,
São José dos Campos, SP 12228-901, Brazil
http://www.ita.br

Abstract. The aim of this paper is to share the main lessons learned in more than one year of work in the Agile Transformation of the Brazilian Aeronautics Computing Center of São José dos Campos. At the beginning of works, the intention was to support the implementation of Scrum as a framework for software development. The first faced challenge was the paradox between Scrum, for its horizontality in the interaction between individuals and the military hierarchy. An update in the Internal Regulations of this Computing Center included in its organizational structure a Project Management Office focused on advising Scrum Teams. The Scrum Teams were also included in the organizational structure, with no hierarchical link to any sector of the Organization. Over time, there has been an increase in people's engagement to this work. The year 2019 began with the reorganization of the teams, following the Scrum Guide, and with two success stories: the construction of a Flight Simulator and the development of a system that controls the overflight of foreign aircraft in brazilian airspace.

Keywords: Agile methods · Scrum · Hierarchy

1 Introduction

The adoption of agile methods at the Brazilian Aeronautics Computing Center of São José dos Campos (Centro de Computação da Aeronáutica de São José dos Campos - CCA-SJ) was an initiative of its systems developers. Scrum was chosen as the development framework. However, at first, the teams did not follow the Agile Manifesto [1]. Scrum teams were not properly formed. The Scrum

Supported by CCA-SJ.

Guide [4] was not known by several team members. There were also problems in the interaction between individuals, as there were conflicts between the military hierarchy and the Agile Principles.

We started the Agile Transformation with an intensive work by 3 Agile Coaches. After the first results in adopting agile methods, confidence of the board of directors increased. In less than a year, the organizational culture was changing and Scrum Teams were performing with success, as we could see in our two project cases. A Project Management Office (PMO) has been created, currently with a staff of 9 members. The planning of projects to be developed in 2019 was based on Scrum and the new teams were formed according to the Scrum Guide.

This article presents the journey of the CCA-SJ in this Agile Transformation. After commencement of the work, two projects were conducted entirely based on agile methods: a Flight Simulator [3] and a software system that controls the overflight of foreign aircrafts in Brazilian airspace [3]. The work being done at CCA-SJ in the adoption of agile methods is a pioneer in the Brazilian Air Force (Força Aérea Brasileira - FAB).

The Internal Regulations was updated in order to include the PMO and the Scrum Teams in the organizational structure of the CCA-SJ. The inclusion of Scrum Teams in FAB's regulations is novelty. The way in which Scrum Teams were inserted in the Internal Regulations favored both technical and support advisory to the teams. There was no hierarchical link between Scrum Teams and any other sectors of the Organization.

This paper shows the last updates on the work begun in 2018, presented at the Brazilian Workshop on Agile Methods (Workshop Brasileiro de Métodos Ágeis - WBMA) that year [5]. The main contributions of this paper are the lessons learned from CCA-SJ's Agile Transformation.

2   Action Plan

De Sa et al. [5] presented an Action Plan and its objectives, in order to mitigate the first problems encountered in the CCA-SJ Agile Transformation to allow the use of Scrum within this strongly hierarchical environment. In this section updates are shown for each of the objectives presented in the plan.

Technical Decisions - in the beginning, decisions within teams were made predominantly based on hierarchy. The main actions taken to favor technical decisions were training Product Owners (PO) and Scrum Masters (SM). The CCA-SJ currently has 7 officers with Scrum.org's Professional Scrum Product Owner (PSPO) certification. The training has helped to better understand Scrum and changed mindsets, regarding decision making within teams.

As for the Scrum Masters, after creation of PMO, people assigned to this office were tasked to act as SM. With this came some needs for training. The initial training was conducted by a commissioned officer from CCA-SJ, with the following certifications: PSPO, Agile Coach, and Professional Scrum Master (PSM I). A bidding process is underway for the certification of 4 Scrum Masters as PSM II.

Appreciation of the Military - the proposal to create a career plan within the CCA-SJ follows the plans for 2019. The most significant changes this year were the formation of all Scrum Teams based on the Scrum Guide and the Internal Regulations update, with the insertion of the Scrum Teams within the CCA-SJ organizational structure. Knowledge and skills mapping work is underway with the Center's personnel. After the consolidation of this work, the next step will be the definition of the career plan.

As for meetings with the staff, weekly meetings are held on Thursdays with a timebox of 1 h. These meetings present the results obtained by the teams, success stories, and relevant news presented in the main media of the FAB. In addition, it was created a culture of publicizing and issuing certificates for major works done by staff.

Satisfaction in Relationship with Superiors - weekly staff meetings have become part of the CCA-SJ routine. They also address relationship issues in the workplace. Several lectures are presented, focusing on a variety topics, including teamwork, success, leadership, among others. After that, relationship with superiors is changing to better.

Internal Communication Problems - the main factors contributing to the resolution of internal communication problems addressed by [5] were the weekly staff meetings and also the meetings held by the Commander of the CCA-SJ with the heads of subdivisions, divisions, and advisories.

Chain of Command Support - within the CCA-SJ, the Commander of the Center and also the head of the Technical Division are engaged in the work related to Agile Transformation. Their participation in weekly meetings and support for the work proposed by the PMO are making this engagement more clear. They are also giving support to the PMO, in order to update other internal regulations.

3   Milestones

This section presents the main events that have occurred since the beginning of the CCA-SJ Agile Transformation work. The milestones from the second half of 2018 are shown at Fig. 1.

May 2018: PMO Implementation Committee - this event has marked the beginning of the work. With the creation of this committee, the search for solutions based upon Agile Methods to improve the relationship in the workplace, internal processes, quality in software development, among others, was institutionalized.

August 2018: Agile Coaches Certification - in August 2018, three officers were trained and certified as Agile Coaches by ICAgile. This milestone was important for the performance of these officers within the teams and for the CCA-SJ.

September 2018: PSPO Certification - in September 2018, the official Scrum.org training for PSPO certification was conducted. Thus, 7 military personnel received this certification, which has increased once more the quality of the teams, regarding the implementation of Agile Methods.

Fig. 1. Milestones from the second half of 2018

October 2018: Participation at WBMA - the presentation of a paper in the 9th WBMA, entitled "Scrum in a Strongly Hierarchical Environment", in October 2018, has allowed the sharing of CCA-SJ's initial experiences with the agile community. As a result, various criticisms and experience exchanges added value to the work in progress.

The milestones from the first half of 2019 are shown at Fig. 2.

January 2019: Scrum Team Reorganization - the Scrum Teams were reorganized, in order to start new projects in the year of 2019. To this end, the new Scrum Teams formation was based on the Scrum Guide.

February 2019: PMO Team Increase - at the beginning, the PMO initially had 3 officers dedicated to its activities. In addition, an officer and a civil servant supported the decisions taken by the PMO. Since February 2019, the PMO team has 9 members, including a psychologyst and a statistician. This multidisciplinarity broadened PMO range of activities and helped to start new works, such as Knowledge Management, Competency Management, obsolescence in software systems developed by the CCA-SJ, among others.

April 2019: Delivery of the C-95M's Fligth Simulator - on April 1st, 2019, the CCA-SJ has delivered a flight simulator for the C-95M aircraft to a Brazilian Air Force Flight Squadron, the 1/5 GAv, headquartered in Natal-RN. This delivery was marked in the history of the CCA-SJ, which until then had only developed software systems. The challenge of developing hardware by using Scrum and integrating it with software has brought much teaching to Computing Center's development teams. This is the first case of success in the Agile Transformation of the CCA-SJ.

April 2019: Participation at Agile Trends - the presentation of the lecture "A 99% cheaper flight simulator: how did the FAB accomplish this by using Scrum?" allowed us to share an innovative experience for the CCA-SJ in developing software-integrated hardware.

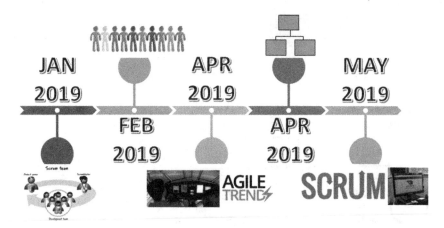

Fig. 2. Milestones from the first half of 2019

April 2019: Internal Regulation Update - the new CCA-SJ Internal Regulation, named RICA 21-183 [2], has inserted the PMO in its organizational structure. In addition, Scrum Teams were institutionalized within the CCA-SJ. An important aspect is that Scrum Teams have no hierarchical link with any sector of the Organization. The main ties of Scrum Teams are: Technical Advisory, with one of the subdivisions from the Technical Division (DT) and Support Advisory, with the PMO.

May 2019: Scrum Trainings at CCA-SJ - with the needs for training the new CCA-SJ Scrum Masters, it was initially decided to perform internal training, prepared by an officer of the Organization itself. With the interest of other CCA military personnel about this training, which was originally planned for 6 people in just 1 class, it was taught to a total of 71 people, divided into 4 classes, including people from other Organizations. This seek for the training has shown the engagement and interest of the CCA-SJ staff in the Agile Transformation work.

May 2019: AVOEM - AVOEM is the name of a system that controls the overflight of foreign aircraft in the brazilian airspace. This project has used Scrum from the beginning until its end. The team introduced the concept of DevOps to the CCA-SJ, that is now being used by all teams. This is considered the second case of success in the Agile Transformation of the CCA-SJ.

The milestones from the beginning of the second half of 2019 are shown at Fig. 3.

August 2019: Lean Inception Training - this training was given to 12 officers, in order to increase the quality of planning for new CCA-SJ projects.

August 2019: Agile Conference - the speak "Agile Adoption in Aeronautics Computing Center of Brazilian Air Force" was presented during the Agile Conference 2019, at Washington-DC, in the Agile in Government track.

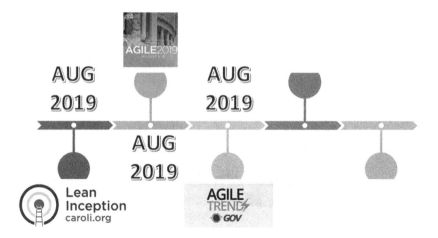

Fig. 3. Milestones from the beginning of the second half of 2019

August 2019: Agile Trends Gov - the lecture entitled "Agile Transformation of an Aeronautics Computing Center" was presented during the largest agility conference in Brazil focused on the public sector.

4   Lessons Learned

This section presents the main Lessons Learned by the PMO team from the CCA-SJ Agile Transformation process.

Transparency is the key to gaining trust - showing to the board of directors in a transparent way what is actually happening with projects is a key factor in gaining trust. In addition, frankly showing the staff what is happening within the Organization increases people's engagement as they start to feel more valued and actually as part of the process. Transparency helped us to deal with most of the problems addressed by [5]. It also has helped to better follow the action plan presented in Sect. 2.

The importance of working top-down and bottom-up approaches simultaneously - in the top-down approach, we work together with the board of directors of the CCA-SJ, showing them the importance of the work being done, with its results. On the other way, working the bottom-up approach empowers the less ranked officers in such way that helps them to contribute with technical decisions to their teams. Transparency also helps significantly in both approaches. Once the board of directors is engaged, there is support from the institution in the process, facilitating the top-down approach. In a bottom-up approach, transformation is facilitated by people's engagement and trust.

Reinforcing the importance of applying Scrum values, principles, and practices - it is not enough to say that one should, for example, hold a daily meeting. It is important that people really understand its meaning and importance. To this end, it should always be appropriate to reinforce the

application of Scrum values, principles, and practices, aiming at its better understanding.

**A case of success becomes an example for other teams and encour-
ages changes that may occur** - a case of success, when shared with other
teams, increases people's engagement. By becoming an example, it makes other
teams seek to repeat the success now achieved. In the case of C-95M's flight simulator, their success in the challenge of integrating software and hardware has
helped other teams to believe in processes, practices, among others. The introduction of DevOps by the AVOEM team has shown other teams a more efficient
way of testing and delivering software. After that, other teams have started to
use the concepts and tools introduced by AVOEM.

5   Final Considerations

The CCA-SJ Agile Transformation continues as a work in progress. Nevertheless,
it is already possible to notice a change in the Organizational Culture.

The objectives set in the Action Plan outlined at the beginning of the work
in 2018 is evolving as its goals are being met.

The milestones presented here show that the CCA-SJ is on the right track.

The lessons learned here have become guides for the steps to come.

For the second half of 2019, new initiatives are expected to be introduced
and internalized in the CCA-SJ, such as DevOps and Lean Inception.

The Upcoming Events that we will participate are Agile Brazil and PSM
II training. During the Agile Brazil 2019, we will present the lecture entitled
"Agile Transformation of an Aeronautics Computing Center". In October 2019,
four officers will participate in official Scrum.org PSM II training.

The authors of this article believe that the lessons learned and reported here
from the agile transformation of the CCA-SJ can be still expanded and may
represent new solutions for old, current, and future problems of any Computing
Center.

References

1. Beck, K., et al.: Manifesto for Agile Software Development (2001). https://
   agilemanifesto.org
2. BRASIL: Regimento Interno do Centro de Computação da Aeronáutica de São José
   dos Campos (2019)
3. Força Aérea Brasileira: NOTAER (2019). https://issuu.com/portalfab/docs
4. Schwaber, K., Sutherland, J.: The scrum guide (2017). https://www.scrum.org/
   resources/scrum-guide
5. de Sá, F.R., de Resende Lucas, E.L., de Oliveira, A.D.: Scrum in a strongly hierarchical organization. In: Tonin, G.S., Estácio, B., Goldman, A., Guerra, E. (eds.)
   WBMA 2018. CCIS, vol. 981, pp. 97–102. Springer, Cham (2019). https://doi.org/
   10.1007/978-3-030-14310-7_7

Agile Experiences in a Software Development Extension Course at a Software Engineering Bachelor's Degree

Carlos Felipe Arantes(✉) ⓘ, Patrícia Lourenço Pereira, Soraia Lúcia da Silva, and Tadeu dos Reis Faria

Pontifícia Universidade Católica de Minas Gerais, Belo Horizonte, Minas Gerais, Brazil
{carlos.arantes,patricia.pereira}@sga.pucminas.br,
{soraialu,tadeurf}@pucminas.br

Abstract. This paper presents the results found in the application and adaptation of an agile approach to software development in a course called "Interdisciplinary Software Project IV" at the bachelor's degree in Software Engineering from the Pontifical Catholic University of Minas Gerais over two years with twenty projects already done. In the fourth semester of the course, students have to develop a software with a social focus. They are introduced to real customers from the communities with real problems and need to incorporate useful knowledge of the current semester subjects into their system, with artifacts and documentation. Through the use of the Scrum framework, it was possible to observe several adaptations made to suit the academic context, although the practical reality of the course, and the nature of the clients for which the projects are developed. Throughout the paper are presented the results obtained and which can serve as an example for similar approaches.

Keywords: Software Engineering · Agile methodology · Interdisciplinary projects · Scrum · Education · Community-driven projects · Extension

1 Introduction

In the Bachelor of Software Engineering (SE) at the Pontifical Catholic University of Minas Gerais (PUC Minas) there is a compulsory course from the first to the sixth semester known as "Interdisciplinary Software Project" (ISP) in which the student must develop a fully functional software following all the development stages, from requirements elicitation to implementation and even maintenance, should a correction be required. For each semester, the current courses are incorporated, enhancing the bachelor with an interdisciplinary character that allows them to practice various concepts given inside the classroom combined with a serious practice with the introduction of clients and real needs. In this way, teachers can guide students through their journeys inside the course by introducing good market practices and raising the status of their work in addressing today's social problems.

P. Meirelles et al. (Eds.): WBMA 2019, CCIS 1106, pp. 92–98, 2019.
https://doi.org/10.1007/978-3-030-36701-5_8

Specifically, the present paper brings the experiences and results of the fourth period ISP (ISP IV) in which 20 software projects have already been developed over two years of application of the course. They are free to choose the technology that they want to work, considering it is in agreement with the requisites. Such languages that have been chosen are: JavaScript, PHP, Java, C #, Python and frameworks such as Express, Zend, Spring and .NET among others; but with the differential of dealing with the chancellor course for the practice of the extension, in which the product realized must solve a problem with a social character.

According to the National Extension Policy [3], one of the advances that deserve attention concerns the institutionalization of extension. In this sense, PUC Minas's extension policy [7] addresses excitingly the importance of extension practices performed by the University, aiming at the development and formation of a society that somehow has barriers in various contexts such as social exclusion, difficulty in accessing knowledge and cultural marginalization. These support initiatives will, in some way, add to the university extension as a whole, improving the quality and management of activities and allowing students to deal with current societal problems generating professional and especially human growth.

In addition to the subjects included in ISP IV and the extension nature, students should develop their respective systems through agile methodology, applying Scrum and adapting it accordingly. Throughout the article, the applied method and the results of the agile approach in the practical academic environment are described.

2 Related Works

Souza, Oliveira, Grillo and Cico [10] bring that by allowing students the possibility to put into practice the techniques studied, given the development of their ability to divide problems, prioritize and establish chronograms; they have been given a huge gain in technical skills, especially in management.

Souza and Pinto [11] bring in their report that the results of the application of an agile methodology were very positive, and a huge development can be perceived in the students throughout the experience. They specifically report that by the simplicity of the agile method, students quickly understood how to work, divide and deliver functionality but that team success correlates with the agile culture present in those involved.

Billa and Cira [12] propose the use of the PBL approach, known as Problem Based Learning for Software Engineering Teaching. In this approach, students solve real problems by applying the concepts of SE, strongly connected to the same approach used with ISP IV.

3 Theoretical Background

It is emphasized in advance that, as it has an extension course too inside the course, a greater work is done on the importance of this type of projects, but at the same time, it is not neglected the application and teaching of processes and methodologies, requirements gathering and development, good software engineering practices and project management. In this section, the frameworks that guided and continue to guide the course as a whole are reported.

3.1 Extension Practices

The university extension practice is one of the ways to develop an academic formation that integrates theory and practice in order to establish a dialogical relationship between systematized knowledge and society, enabling knowledge exchange between both. This is mainly because, in extension, it is expected that there will be an academic gain for the institution, that is, the actions developed will be internalized as methodological tests for community work, knowledge of real society problems, professional experience for teachers and students, development of procedures and technical standards; in short, a two-way street for everyone involved.

The actions of this extension practice that is presented broaden the classroom space, allowing the exchange of knowledge within and outside the academic environment and also contributes to the renewal of pedagogical processes through exchange and participation between internal and external communities to the university, which strengthens the University Extension Policy of PUC Minas [7]. The activities carried out in this work contribute to the PUC Minas Institutional Development Plan [8] in enabling students to articulate the theory of the current semester with the vivid experience, allowing also a direct contact with society contributing to a more humane and citizen formation; and are part of the Pedagogical Project of the Software Engineering course. Working with extension practices allows the teachers involved to rethink their activities (action-reflection - action), improving their knowledge and methodologies.

Regarding the students, it can be said that society has been demonstrating the need for a higher educated professional who has a more complete education, not only technical but also ethical, humanistic and cultural, who can work with other areas in multidisciplinary teams. Thus, the participation of students in these practices contributes to them acting in society with competence, responsibility and justice, contributing to the construction of a prosperous, solidary and fair country.

3.2 Agile Methodologies and Scrum

The ISP subject, in line with the latest practices adopted in the market, emerges students into contact with agile methodologies. The Agile Manifesto, the artifact that defines these methodologies, makes it clear that the valorization of individuals and interactions is prioritized over the use of processes and tools, which makes the main objective to build software over its documentation. To achieve this, customer collaboration throughout the development becomes more necessary than contract negotiation, and the team must be better prepared to respond to changes than following a plan [1]. Agile methods tend to refer to source code as the sole documentation artifact [4], with the aim of solving the problem of creating high quality software being built in a timely manner in the face of constantly changing requirements in the business environment, bringing the need for the development team to be adaptive and able to cope with changing requirements at any stage of development [5].

The most commonly used agile method among students is SCRUM, a structural framework based on empirical process control theories, which has been widely used to manage the development of complex products since the early 1990s [9]. It employs an iterative and incremental approach to improve predictability and risk control.

The widely used SCRUM artifacts and events are Product Backlog, Sprint Backlog and Sprint [2], the latter having a fixed time period, which can be from two to four weeks. For the subject in question, teachers guide students through two-week Sprints, which consist of Sprint Planning, Daily Scrum Meetings, development work, Sprint Review, and Sprint Retrospective. Within this range, the software increment is built and delivered by students, starting a new Sprint immediately after the previous one.

The SCRUM roles are Product Owner (PO), Scrum Master (SM) and Dev Team (DT), which constitutes the "Time Scrum" [9]. The PO is responsible for maximizing product value and managing Product Backlog. The DT is staffed by professionals who do the job of delivering a potentially reliably incremental "ready-made" product at the end of each Sprint, which is required by the Sprint Review. SM is responsible for constantly promoting framework knowledge by helping everyone understand the theory, practices, rules and values of the methodology, helping to maximize the value created by DT.

Through the concepts introduced by the method, teams should be multifunctional and self-organizing, bringing flexibility, creativity and productivity to the team, as well as making the team not dependent on others outside the DT or dependent solely on what is needed to develop the project and make decisions.

3.3   Interdisciplinary Software Project IV

Interdisciplinary Software Project IV (ISP IV) - course of the Department of Software Engineering and Information Systems at PUC Minas - was approved as the extension course of the Software Engineering bachelor's degree at PUC Minas. Its function is to articulate the contents of the other courses of the fourth semester around the development of social-minded application software. The subject of software development should meet the perceptions of social need diagnosed by the Extension Coordination department, coordinator of the bachelor, or the demands of developing programs and applications from University extension projects. In this case, 34 h are computed in the valorization of the extension in the course [6].

This course is fundamental for the student to practice the extension activities and to understand the humanistic foundations aimed by PUC Minas and dealt with in the pedagogical project of the course. The objective is to promote the transformative interaction of the course with other sectors of society, constituting an indispensable component for the formation of students and teacher qualification. The extension actions of this course also consider the inseparability with Teaching and Research. In the interface with the research, the methodology incorporates investigative practice. In articulation with teaching the process happens through the mediating action between theory and practice.

Also, it integrates, through practical bias, knowledge of other courses of the period and several others taught in previous periods, thus promoting their interdisciplinary content. It contributes to the formation of the egress profile, as it enables the student to develop skills and abilities to assess real needs or problems with socially-oriented software in the form of observing the actions/work routine of the community through interviews (dialogued interaction) with the society, potential users and stakeholders.

The goal for the teacher is to identify potential problem situations in the community that can be solved through a software solution and to enable students to assess needs or requirements for a socially based computational solution in the form of observing the routine actions/work of a community. The goal for the student is to develop the ability to dialogue with the client and users to gather requirements and user profile identification, besides the development of the solution itself. The goal for the community is to identify with the teacher possible problem situations and provide students with details of the problem that will serve as the basis for defining the requirements of social application software that can solve a specific community problem.

4 Methodology

Following are the steps of the work methodology used throughout the semesters to date in the course: (1) Identify potential communities, non-profit organizations and projects for society given the existence of problems that can be solved via software product. For example, these communities may be existing NGOs that have well-defined social objectives and need to record their actions through some software; (2) Prepare students to conduct requirements gathering in the form of observation and documentation of the community's work routine and dialogued interview with their stakeholders. At this time, the teacher prepares students for a sympathetic perception of the reality of the community by embracing their cause to provide their contributions. The character of humanistic formation of this course is fundamental here. This software will be made by people for people. The technological component of the software is secondary to the needs of organizations and society; (3) Visit the community to conduct an interview with potential users of the software, also identifying the user profile (comfort level with technology, ease/difficulty in handling applications on the computer). The purpose of the interview is to raise the software requirements and the needs of this community in front of informatization. The person responsible for the entity will also be invited to attend the classroom for a brief presentation of the organization and its demands; (4) Describe/specify the requirements raised by creating the so-called software specification documents; (5) Validate the document with the community or a prototype. Where also demonstrated and explained the relationship with Scrum. This stage is already a proposal for intervention in the community routine and needs community validation. (6) Design and implement the software described in the Software Requirements Specification Document that has been validated by the community; (7) Present the software to the community for evaluation, and correction of possible defects and minor adjustments. At this moment, the intervention proposal is implemented. If the community accepts the intervention, it will use the software; (8) Perform usability testing with real users to identify improvement points for the software. It is important to note that these activities are developed in an interdisciplinary manner in the fourth period.

With the introduction of artifacts in Scrum, the Sprints were defined with an average of fifteen days each, and students are given greater attention - and as a consequence directly reflected in the grade obtained in the course - regarding the application of: (1) the methodology and its artifacts; (2) the participation of the customer or their Product Owner throughout the process; (3) the well-executed division of tasks. It is because of the nature of the course that students are given a greater attention to good software engineering practices and therefore a considerable part of the project development is closely connected to the techniques and to a correct and validated documentation approach. - following agile principles - of the software.

Weekly students meet with one or more teachers of the course to explain the difficulties encountered and are guided by these teachers on how to correct the deviations. In addition, the teachers choose the backlog of each Sprint, given the scope of each system individually. For each item prioritized for Sprint, the acceptance criteria set by the teachers and the clients are validated. All monitoring of the project is carried out through project management and control tools by both the teachers and the students. It is important emphasize that the follow-up is constant. Incomplete, failed or nonexistent use of agile methodology artifacts is considered as a review point to be worked with students throughout all the reserved classes for the follow-up.

5 Results

The course uses software development cycle planning mechanisms that contribute to: (1) the enrichment of teamwork skills, fostering the distribution of responsibilities and collaboration, whether with clients or teammates, based on software models, both through written and oral communication; (2) work in a team; (3) lead teams and deal with people from different realities; (4) allow students to self-evaluate and evaluate their pairs and develop characteristics favorable to interpersonal relationships; (5) enables the decision-making exercise on the appropriate selection of technologies for the software solution and the development of creative and innovative solutions, since it generates a relationship of trust with the customer; (6) It also gives students the opportunity to play different roles, as they are, at different times, developers, consultants, moderators, reviewers, researchers, instructors, technical leaders and project managers. Behold, the student himself stimulates the development of his autonomy, driving the creation of business-focused planning, through an application chosen by the group, always focusing on the research of market demands and with a more humane look in the proposal of solutions considering social realities.

Students are assessed and scored according to the documents and functionalities produced: (1) Software Specification Document; (2) Socially oriented solution; Software usability testing report by its end-users; (3) Reports proposed by PROEX, responsible for extension zeal at PUC Minas, through the Extension Course Management tool. And, at the end of the course, students complete an extension practice assessment form consisting of eleven questions and can choose from the following answers: strongly disagree, partially disagree, undecided, partially agree, totally agree, or not applicable. Approximately 86% totally agreed that the practice allowed the students to value the exchange of knowledge between the University and other sectors of society. About 71% fully agreed that it was possible to build new knowledge from the challenges presented in practice; 70% totally agreed that acting in practice made possible the integration of models, concepts and methodologies from various areas of knowledge. Approximately 79% fully agreed that it was possible to exercise ethical posture and respect for diversity. About 71% fully agreed that the work carried out made it possible to verify the social relevance of the profession, to be attentive to social, regional or local development. Over 70% fully agreed that they learned to articulate theory with lived practice, developing professional skills and competences.

It is also noteworthy that throughout the semesters, there was a need for teachers to take the roles of Product Owner and Scrum Master, given the distance from real customers and the possible impediments caused by it. For this, teachers need to become better acquainted with each client's domains, the condition they are in and the needs of each one; they become a bridge to resolve conflicts and bottlenecks with clients. But even so, the students also incorporate some of this role of PO, given that due to the volume of groups it does not allow very specific attention to a particular group, being an unnecessary control, but which makes room for the student to develop autonomy and initiative. It was also noted that the students had a high acceptance with the introduction of technologies for managing their tasks such as Trello, Jira, Asana and Kanban among others allowing them to deal with project management at an early beginning.

At the end of the work, the application is tested and evaluated by the community, which is also invited to participate in the final presentation of the project together with the bachelor's faculty. Almost 100% of the partners have approved the developed systems, including the importance of the tool in achieving the daily activities of each organization and in the transformative power that information technology plays in the current century making the students trained by the coursed aware of the responsibility they carry in building the future.

References

1. Beck, K., et al.: Manifesto for agile software development. Agil. Alliance 2009 (2001). 2006
2. CIENT, Interinstitucional Editor et al.: Difficulties in the Adoption and Use of Scrum Method in Brazilian Companies. As Dificuldades na Adoção e Uso de Método Scrum em Empresas Brasileiras Utilizando Processos Plan-Driven: Estudo de Caso Múltiplo, vol. 8, pp. 66–79 (2017)
3. Extension Forum of rectors of the Brazilian public universities. National University Extension Policy, Manaus, Brasil (2012)
4. Fraga, B.S., Barbosa, M.W.: Requirements engineering in agile methods: a systematic literature review. In: XIII Brazilian Symposium on Information Systems, June 2017, pp. 309–315 (2017)
5. De Lucia, A., Qusef, A.: Requirements engineering in agile software development. J. Emerg. Technol. Web Intell. 2(3), 212–221 (2010)
6. Pontifícia Universidade Católica de Minas Gerais: Pedagogical project of the Computer Engineering degree (2017)
7. Pontifícia Universidade Católica de Minas Gerais: University Extension Policy of PUC Minas. PUC Minas/Pró-Reitoria de Extensão, Belo Horizonte (2006)
8. Pontifícia Universidade Católica de Minas Gerais: Institutional Development Plan: 2012 to 2016. PUC Minas, Belo Horizonte (2011)
9. Schwaber, K., Sutherland, J.: Scrum Guide: The Definitive Guide to Scrum (2017)
10. Souza, S., Oliveira, B., Grillo, F., Cico, C.: Building digital platforms while teaching Software Engineering: an experience report. IX Software Engineering Education Forum. Fees (2016)
11. Souza, S., Pinto, V.: Building social applications while teaching software engineering: an experience report. Third Congress of Graduation from São Paulo University. USP (2017)
12. Billa, C.Z., Cera, M.C.: Using problem solving to approximate theory and practice in software engineering. V Software Engineering Education Forum. Fees (2012)

Agile Practices

Identifying Success Factors in a Legacy Systems Reengineering Project Using Agile Methods

Everton Mateus Fernandes[(⊠)] and Thiago Schumacher Barcelos

Laboratório de Computação Aplicada – LABCOM3, Instituto Federal de Educação,
Ciência e Tecnologia de São Paulo, Guarulhos, São Paulo, Brazil
`everton.mfernandes@gmail.com, tsbarcelos@ifsp.edu.br`

Abstract. System maintenance or extension costs, during its lifecycle, can exceed the cost of its rewriting and can lead companies to choose a reengineering strategy. On the other hand, several similarities between recommended practices for reengineering projects and agile practices can be found in the literature. Hence, this article aims to understand the success factors that influence the reengineering process of legacy systems and how agile methods can influence the results. A real project of a software development company in the city of Sao Paulo was used as basis for a case study of a legacy system reengineering to a SOA application. The project results were compared with the perception of the development team through semi-structured interviews, the analysis of project artifacts and the best practices proposed in the literature to understand whether the results mentioned in the literature would be confirmed in practice. The obtained results reinforce the hypothesis that reengineering projects can be more successful when developed using agile methodologies.

Keywords: Software reengineering · Agile methods

1 Introduction

Legacy software systems are maintained as long as their maintenance and evolution costs outweigh the replacement or rewriting costs. The cost of maintaining or extending a system can increase due to several factors, but we can highlight architectural, documentation, design or granularity problems of its components [1, 2]. All of these factors over time can lead to a high cost of maintenance or impossibility to implement extensions and, therefore, lead to the decision to abandon the system, rewrite it or reengineer it.

The reengineering process involves understanding a legacy system and redeploying its functionality in order to improve the quality of functional and non-functional requirements [1]. The reasons for adopting a system reengineering approach can be diverse as time/cost to create a new system, knowledge added to the existing product, adherence to the company's business, among others [2]. Thus, the system reengineering process aims to rebuild the system in a new form to make its maintenance and extension costs more sustainable.

© Springer Nature Switzerland AG 2019
P. Meirelles et al. (Eds.): WBMA 2019, CCIS 1106, pp. 101–110, 2019.
https://doi.org/10.1007/978-3-030-36701-5_9

The system reengineering process can be done iteratively, going through cycles of requirements gathering, risk assessment, new system engineering and results evaluation [1, 3]. In addition to the iterative and incremental cycle, several standards are proposed in the literature for this process [1–3].

Iterative and incremental development processes have gained strength in the industry with the adoption of agile project management and system development methodologies. The main gains of these methodologies are the ability to deliver continuous value, flexibility to change, increased confidence in code through automated testing, among others [4].

In this article we present the results of a reengineering project of part of a legacy Enterprise Resource Planning (ERP) system, developed and distributed by a software development company based on São Paulo, Brazil as a case study to understand how the reengineering practices and agile methodologies proposed in the literature affected the project outcome. A literature review was conducted to find reported best practices and success factors for both reengineering projects and projects using agile methods. In Sect. 2, related works and main concepts applied in the study are presented. In order to understand the application of the practices proposed in the literature, Sect. 3 will detail the project, then Sect. 4 will present the interview data, Sect. 5 will show an analysis of documental data and Sect. 6 will discuss project results through triangulation between literature data, team perceptions obtained through interviews and document analysis. Finally, Sect. 7 will present the conclusions of the study.

2 Related Works

2.1 Systems Reengineering

The reengineering process involves understanding a legacy system and redeploying its functionality to improve functional and non-functional requirements [1]. To achieve the expected results, the legacy system goes through the reverse engineering processes of the application and subsequent reimplementation of its requirements.

Khadka *et al.* [5] searched for reengineering models in the literature and found variations of Plan, Do, Check and Act (PDCA) software development models focused on the reengineering process. This process works in an iterative way, starting with understanding the legacy software, designing the intended software, performing a feasibility study and then going through cycles of choosing and applying migration, implementation and deployment techniques.

Reengineering projects have factors in common which have been identified as success factors raised from case studies [6]. Among them we can highlight:

- Legacy system potential: Complexity, documentation, testing, code quality, and access to undocumented legacy information influence the reengineering process.
- Migration strategy: The strategy should be chosen taking into consideration financial, technical and people resources. Techniques include covering old code with new services, rewriting the logic of a monolithic system into smaller services, among others.

- Company business process: Company engagement for the project is very important, as usually some stakeholders are at the top hierarchical levels and have the necessary influence to drive the project forward. Therefore it is important for reengineering to be aligned with business needs to show value in the proposed deliverables and not just rewrite the code.
- Budget and Resources: Depending on the size of the legacy, proposed systems change, and business impact, the reengineering process can take more or less time, and financial, technical, and human resources are keys to give body and structure to the continuity of the project.
- Constant monitoring of the migration process: Monitoring committees and periodic process reviews help keep the project course in line with company expectations and even allow direction changes when needed.
- Testing: In the legacy system they help to document functionality and in the new application they help to validate and guarantee deliveries in terms of performance, reliability and safety.
- Team technical skills: The team's technical level can directly impact on time and quality of delivery, since it may be necessary for the team to acquire new knowledge and expertise during the project.

2.2 Agile Methods, Practices, and Success Factors

Melo *et al.* [7] and Mazuco [8] identified through structured interviews the most widely used agile methods in the Brazilian software industry and listed Scrum and a mixed version of Scrum and XP as the most commonly used methodologies and daily meeting, unit testing, sprint planning, product backlog and release planning as the most adopted practices. In the mentioned works there is also consensus that the adoption of agile practices brings improvements such as increased productivity, better adaptability to changes, improved team communication and increased quality of delivered software.

Through a systematic literature review [9] 14 factors that influence the success of projects using agile methods were identified. These factors were divided into 3 categories and can be seen in Table 1.

Table 1. Factors that influence the success of agile projects

People	Processes	Technology
Competence and Expertise	Agile Practices	Appropriate Technical Training
Executive Support	Deliver key functionality first	Tests (Unit, Integration, etc.)
Team and user motivation	The right amount of documentation	Simple Design
Small Teams	Strong Communication	Tooling Support
User Participation		Well-defined coding standards

3 Case Study

In order to confront the practices proposed in the literature with a real application, this article gathered data from a reengineering project of part of a legacy Enterprise Resource Planning (ERP) system, developed and distributed by a software development company based on São Paulo, Brazil. The case study was chosen as the research strategy; according to Wholin et al. [10], this strategy is suitable for studying phenomena in real contexts and also for confronting the obtained results with earlier studies or theories. The same authors argue that analysis of multiple sources of information is important to ensure the validity of the results. Hence, for project analysis, a triangulation strategy [11] was used to confront literature data, documental analysis of project artifacts (Jira, Git, etc.) and semi-structured interviews with those involved in the development phase.

The company's legacy product consisted of a Client × Server application and a web portal. The solution could be installed in a customer-owned environment (On Premise), in a cloud provider infrastructure as a service (IaaS), or through software as a service (SaaS) model provided by the software company. The backend and web services used on the legacy system's web portal were written in the company's proprietary language using a structured paradigm. Application code was shared across the entire ERP system, which made it difficult to scale specific services. The frontend mainly used pure Javascript with Bootstrap for validations and building interface components.

After analyzing the difficulties generated by the complexity of the legacy product, the company compared the costs involved and potential benefits of legacy maintenance and chose to reengineer part of the application by creating a new product based on a fully service oriented architecture (SOA), offering it only as SaaS hosted by a third-party vendor. The new product was still written in the same proprietary language but using the object-oriented paradigm. Specifically, standalone ERP-isolated services were developed, providing individual scalability. Webservices stopped using SOAP and started using REST following OpenAPI standards. For the frontend a framework based on Angular 2 was used and the interface was completely redesigned to improve usability.

The expected gains at the start of the project were: improved code quality; a more robust system architecture, creating an application that is easier to administer and deploy; decreased concurrency between application functionalities, and to create a independent product that could be offered without the need to purchase the entire ERP.

The team was initially composed of 3 middle level developers, 1 Product Owner and was subordinate to 1 product manager. At the time of writing, the team had 5 developers, 1 DevOps analyst, 1 Tester, 1 Scrum Master and was under duties of 1 product manager and 1 engineering manager. During the project 3 developers were relocated to other demands. The project started in July 2017 and lasted about 20 months, being one month to initial understanding of the problem and 19 months to development. The initial understanding phase served to understand the project needs and validate with customers whether the proposed solution would be appropriate to them. For that, a Design Sprint week was held, high fidelity prototypes were created and the minimum viable product (MVP) validated with the customers. In the development phase, initial Sprints 1 through 5 were used to understand the legacy software code, design the classes that would be used as the basis for the backend and to design and develop interfaces based on validated prototypes with customers. From Sprint 6 on the features development began. At Sprint 13, with the input of a DevOps analyst, the production environment began to be prepared to receive the application. Following the start of testing in an environment nearest to production, defects and corrections began to be recorded from Sprint 19. The project matured and at Sprint 26, which took place in November 2017, the pilot project was carried out in first customer. With the pilot's success the system went into production and new features continued to be implemented in the product. New integrations and maintenance actions were also registered.

4   Interviews

After 35 project sprints a semi-structured interview was conducted through an online form with some of those involved in the development phase to understand the agile and reengineering practices used and their impacts on the project from the team's point of view. Then, the content was grouped by similarity of themes using content analysis [11]. The interviews were answered by the Product Owner and 4 developers. The main questions are listed in Table 2, and the full content of the interviews can be accessed at http://bit.ly/2lvUZDZ. Nine recurring themes were identified in the interviews, which are presented below in Table 3.

Table 2. Main questions of the interview.

Q1 - What strategy was adopted to revitalize the legacy system?
Q2 - How good is the legacy system architecture?
Q3 - Did the team have all the skills and technical knowledge at the beginning of the project? How was the knowledge acquisition during the project?
Q4 - How was the project management support?
Q5 - How was the pilot user accepting the project idea and after implementation?
Q6 - How did the team grow or shrink during the project? How did this impact throughout the process?
Q7 - How was the user participation in the project decision making?
Q8 - Which agile practices have been adopted?
Q9 - How did agile practices contribute to the success of the project?
Q10 - How the application was documented? Is there documentation requested by the customer?
Q12 - How did team communication influence the project?
Q13 - What types of tests were applied? Has this practice given safety and quality to the product?
Q14 - How complex is the design of the end application?
Q15 - What is the toolset used in the application development, maintenance and deployment process? How did this tooling evolve?
Q16 - Are coding standards defined? How does this help in the project?

Table 3. Themes found in interviews

Theme	Citation examples
Learning throughout the project	Learning a new framework
Legacy issues and difficulties	Complex code, lack of documentation
Legacy strengths	Business rule adherence
Using reengineering practices	Legacy code study, rules extraction
Use of agile practices	Sprint planning, pair programming
Good management support	Team autonomy
Project difficulties	New developers adapt
Project gains	More stable product

Agile practices were well accepted by the team and were perceived positively. As key benefits the team cited improved communication, close contact with the customer, functionality deliveries that add customer value. The most mentioned practices are presented below in Table 4.

Table 4. Most mentioned agile practices

Architectural spikes/spike solutions	Retrospectives
Version control	Demonstration or review meeting
Definition of done	Daily meeting
Frequent deliveries	Code review
Product backlog	Scrum master
Task board	Sprint backlog
Refactoring	TDD

The use of a proprietary programming language and the adoption of the Object Oriented paradigm were seen as an initial hindering factor for learning; on the other hand, coding standards and automated test cases were pointed out as facilitators of knowledge transmission and helped, in the team's perception, to reduce the time between the developer's entry and the start of his work on the project. In addition, the team had to deal with a completely new architecture by company standards. This required several stories of study.

The team considered that the product was easy and intuitive for the end user, due to the fact that, without training, after the pilot, about 200 users were accessing the product in a fluid manner and with no maintenance usability issues.

Another perception of the team is that now it is easier to implement new features and maintain the product. Automated testing brought more security to perform code maintenance and refactoring. Serious production problems are rarely encountered and the tests help to guarantee that the new sprint deploy won't break the code or process in production.

5   Document Analysis

As an indicator of the evolution of team deliveries we used the number of commits performed per month, shown in Fig. 1, and the amount of points delivered by Sprint presented in Fig. 2.

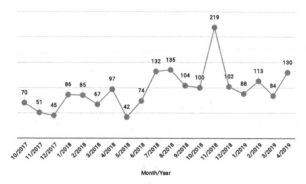

Fig. 1. Commits by month/year

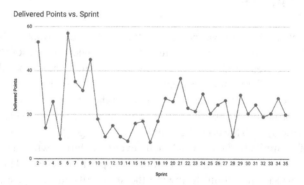

Fig. 2. Delivered Points vs Sprint

We gathered data about the movement of team members with the product owner of the project. Movement data included active people who joined and left the project and people who were on vacation. The graph showing this movement is shown in Fig. 3.

Figure 4 shows the evolution of the number of test cases. The quantity of test cases present at the end of each sprint was gathered from the version control repository.

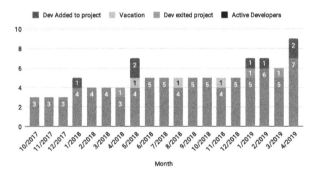

Fig. 3. Staff variation per month

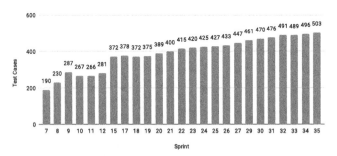

Fig. 4. Number of test cases per Sprint

6   Analysis of Results

In the test case chart (Fig. 4) we can notice that developers adopted the creation of automated testing as a practice and continued to develop new test cases throughout the project. This practice was cited in the interviews as a positive factor; besides this, it is a recommended practice for both reengineering [6] and agile methods [9].

In some interview excerpts it was mentioned that the change and departure of developers affected the project progress, this can be reinforced by comparing the staff variation chart by month (Fig. 3) with the commit chart by month (Fig. 1), where there is a decrease in the number of commits in the months when developers left or when a developer went on vacation. It is worth noting that the commit chart per month (Fig. 1) tends to return to the previous level in the month following the staff exit, thus suggesting that a new developer adaptation time tends to last about one month. This was considered a short time by the team. The short adaptation time may have contributed to keeping the number of points delivered by mid-sprints to the end of the project stable even with 4 new developers coming in and 2 leaving in the last 3 months of the project as seen in Fig. 2.

In the commit chart by month (Fig. 1) it is possible to observe a peak of commits in November that coincides with the pilot project showing that the team had a different approach during this period to support the demands of the project in production, but soon the demand normalized, thus suggesting that the project in production remains stable and does not have high demands for maintenance, a suggestion also made by those involved in the interviews.

Based on the practices proposed in the literature, we can identify common factors between software reengineering and agile practices. Technical expertise, testing, management support and simple design are factors mentioned in both methodologies and were present in this reengineering project according to the interviewees. In this project, we could see many factors that helped the good results indicated by the team. Some of them are: choosing a migration strategy in initial sprints to support the knowledge extraction from legacy code; the presence of executive support, budget and resources to execute the project and alignment with the company's business process; constant monitoring of the migration process with scrum ceremonies and agile practices; applying testing practices from the beginning; team and user motivation with constant user participation; organization of small teams; delivering of key functionality first; producing only the necessary amount of documentation; usage of strong communication to align expectations and learn from each other; providing technical training during the project; producing a simple design; usage of tooling support and well-defined coding standards. Despite that, some difficulties were also found because the legacy system was hard to maintain, extract information and test, did not have automated tests or good documentation. However, the migration strategy was effective enough to get the knowledge from the source code. The competence and expertise had to be obtained during the processed supported by agile practices, and this made the project run slower than expected.

7 Conclusions

Given the similarity between a subset of successful practices in agile and reengineering projects, as well as the suggestion to organize reengineering processes in an iterative and incremental fashion, it is valid to suppose that reengineering projects tend to be most successful when developed using agile methodologies. Thus, it is also possible to conclude that the success factors of agile projects, such as technical expertise, simple design, testing, among others, can also positively affect reengineering projects. This hypothesis is preliminarily supported by case studies such as that presented by Galinium and Shahbaz [6], which identified a demand for high level of communication, visibility of progress and adaptation to change when necessary in reengineering processes. In the case study presented in this article, based on the analyzed data we found evidence that agile methods in fact supported the execution of the reengineering strategy, as they allowed the team to acquire and disseminate knowledge throughout the project through spike practices, team lectures for team and pair programming. In addition, agile practices served to ensure that business and customer needs were met from the outset of the project and that customer demands were constantly prioritized.

The reengineering project was considered successful from the customer's point of view, as identified through testimonials given to the development team and mentioned in the interviews. The reengineered system provided better performance and more stability. From the development team's point of view, the application now has better code quality and easier maintenance and development of new features. For the company, the developed product is aligned with its strategy and meets the needs of its customer. The project results helps to reinforce the hypothesis that reengineering projects can be more successful when developed using agile methodologies.

References

1. Demeyer, S., Ducasse, S., Nierstrasz, O.: Reengineering patterns. In: Object-Oriented Reengineering Patterns, pp. 1–14. Elsevier (2003). https://doi.org/10.1016/B978-155860639-5/50006-7
2. Majthoub, M., Qutqui, M.H., Odeh, Y.: Software re-engineering: an overview. In: 2018 8th International Conference on Computer Science and Information Technology (CSIT), Amman, pp. 266–270. IEEE (2018). https://doi.org/10.1109/CSIT.2018.8486173
3. Sahoo, A., Kung, D., Gupta, S.: An agile methodology for reengineering object-oriented software. Presented at the 28th International Conference on Software Engineering and Knowledge Engineering, 1 July 2016. https://doi.org/10.18293/SEKE2016-227
4. 13th Annual State of Agile Report. https://www.stateofagile.com/#ufh-i-521251909-13th-annual-state-of-agile-report/473508
5. Khadka, R., Saeidi, A., Idu, A., Jurrian, H., Jansen, S.: Legacy to SOA Evolution: A Systematic Literature Review. IGI Global, Hershey (2012)
6. Galinium, M., Shahbaz, N.: Success factors model: case studies in the migration of legacy systems to Service Oriented Architecture. In: 2012 Ninth International Conference on Computer Science and Software Engineering (JCSSE), Bangkok, Thailand, pp. 236–241. IEEE (2012). https://doi.org/10.1109/JCSSE.2012.6261958
7. de O. Melo, C., et al.: The evolution of agile software development in Brazil: education, research, and the state-of-the-practice. J. Braz. Comput. Soc. **19**, 523–552 (2013). https://doi.org/10.1007/s13173-013-0114-x
8. Mazuco, A.S. da C.: Percepções de Práticas Ágeis em Desenvolvimento de Software: Benefícios e Desafios (2017)
9. da Silva, K.M.B., dos Santos, S.C.: Critical factors in agile software projects according to people, process and technology perspective. In: 2015 6th Brazilian Workshop on Agile Methods (WBMA), Pernambuco, Brazil, pp. 48–54. IEEE (2015). https://doi.org/10.1109/WBMA.2015.19
10. Wholin, C.P.R., Höst, M., Ohlsson, M., Regnell, B., Wesslön, A.: Experimentation in Software Engineering: An Introduction. Kluwer Academic Publishers, New York (2000)
11. Creswell, J.W., Miller, D.L.: Determining validity in qualitative inquiry. Theory Pract. **39**, 124–130 (2000). https://doi.org/10.1207/s15430421tip3903_2

ATIMO – A Tool for Alocating Agile Teams

Júnea Eliza Brandão Caldeira[1,2] , Bruno Rafael de Oliveira Rodrigues[1] ,
Sérgio Roberto Imaeda Yoshioka[2] , and Fernando Silva Parreiras[1(✉)]

[1] Laboratory for Advanced Information Systems - LAIS, Faculty of Business
Sciences, FUMEC University, 30310-190 Belo Horizonte, MG, Brazil
fernando.parreiras@fumec.br
[2] TOTVS S.A., Av. Raja Gabáglia, 2664 - Estoril,
Belo Horizonte, MG 30494-170, Brazil
http://www.fumec.br/lais
http://www.totvs.com.br

Abstract. It is essential for the success of a project to put together
teams that meet the project requirements with lower cost and higher
quality. Given this context, the present study developed a tool called
ATIMO that uses the optimization algorithms *NSGAII*, *SPEA2*, and
MOCell, to put agile teams together. The algorithms implemented in
ATIMO were tested by being applied to four real projects in an experiment performed by a software development company. This approach
took into account the project features, the developers' profile, and both
the project and the organization constraints. As a result, the algorithms
returned solutions with the number of resources needed to carry out
the project as well as the best qualified resources for the project with
productivity and lower cost to meet the established deadline. The algorithms *NSGAII*, and *SPEA2* presented similar results and behavior, as
the *MOCell* algorithm presented a better performance in computational
effort and required a larger population for its saturation.

Keywords: Human resources allocation · Multi-objective
optimization · Agile teams

1 Introduction

The allocation of resources is a critical task in software projects [4]. The decision of the project manager concerning the composition of a team that will work
on a given project may lead to the project either succeeding or failing. This
resource allocation task has aspects that must be pondered according to the
needs of the organization and the project [3], such as the skills, capacities and
experiences of each team member. However, since this is a complex and arduous
task, project managers tend to put together teams that do not satisfy the needs
and demands of a project [3]. In this regard, it becomes relevant that software
development companies increase their efficiency, productivity, and reduce their

P. Meirelles et al. (Eds.): WBMA 2019, CCIS 1106, pp. 111–127, 2019.
https://doi.org/10.1007/978-3-030-36701-5_10

costs [1]. In order to reach these goals, it is essential to properly manage the resources assessing the performance of the teams [10]. By utilizing agile methodologies the work is handled collaboratively, and the teams are self-organized, being able to dynamically adapt to changes in the customer requirements [12].

The composition of a team can be defined based on the view of managers, who may not often consider each team member in terms of knowledge, abilities, attitude, performance, and cost. When the goal is to analyze teams, the process, the product, the organization, and human factors related to the project [13] should be taken into account. As of the mapping of the team's competences, their profile, the managers and project leaders need to evaluate the allocation of the teams as well as allocation to new projects, allowing the companies to enhance the effectiveness and assertiveness of their projects.

It is possible to find studies in literature that use genetic algorithms that enable an automatized process of allocation of resources and assist managers in putting together their teams [5,17]. In this context, this study aims at proposing a tool that supports managers in composing agile teams. Thus, the ATIMO tool was developed utilizing the NSGA II, SPEA2, and MOCELL algorithms as options for putting a team together. With the purpose of measuring the performance of ATIMO, an experiment was conducted in a software development company to make teams with higher quality and lower cost in three real company scenarios.

The present study is structured as follows: Sect. 2 shows the related works, in Sect. 3 there is the modelling of the problem, Sect. 4 presents the algorithms used for building the tool, Sect. 5 contemplates the steps of the experiment, Sect. 6 presents and discusses the results, and finally, Sect. 8 brings the conclusions.

2   Related Work

This study extends the work of Brito *et al.* [5] in 2012 that proposed an approach to solve multi-objective problems by combining optimization methods based on *Search Based Software Engineering* (SBSE). To handle the problem of allocation in agile teams, they utilized the NSGAII multi-objective meta-heuristic algorithm and the Mandani Fuzzy inference system. In the present study the ATIMO tool was implemented based on the approach proposed by Brito *et al.*, but unlike them, the SPEA2 and MOCell algorithms were also used.

Nebro *et al.* propose the MOCell algorithm for solving multi-objective optimization problems and compare its performance to the NSGA-II and SPEA2 [2] algorithms. A novel cellular genetic algorithm was introduced to solve multi-objective optimization problems. The idea was to assess problems with or without constraints and compare them to two state-of-the-art evolutionary multi-objective optimizers, NSGA-II and SPEA2. The experiment carried out with ATIMO in this work indicated that MOCell obtained more competitive results in terms of convergence and hypervolume and overcame the two algorithms compared as of the diversity of the solutions along the Pareto chart.

Connor and Shah [7] presented the results of the application of three meta-heuristic search algorithms in solving problems in project management software.

The *Simulated annealing, tabu search* algorithm and genetic algorithms were assessed in problems regarding allocation and setting out resources [7]. The objective of this research was to measure the performance of different techniques of meta-heuristic search regarding typical problems of software development projects when allocating and setting out resources *software*. In the present study, we report a tool that uses genetic algorithms to solve allocations problems and a set of experiments that measure the performance of three studied algorithms and the results point out that all of the heuristic research techniques can be used to solve problems when allocating and putting resources together for a software project. The comparative analysis suggested that the genetic algorithm performed better than the other two algorithms in the study. Thus, differently from Connor and Shah, this study dealt with selecting the human resources, assigning them project tasks, that is, allocated the resources in the project.

3   Modelling the Problem

The solution to the problem is modelled as binary vectors in which:

- The size of the vector is the same size as of the pool of the analysts.
- 0 or 1 in a position of the vector represents whether the analyst in that position is present or absent.

The problem has two objective functions to minimize the cost and maximize the competences described in Eqs. 1 and 2. They are inspired by the study of Brito et al. [5].

$$Min \sum_{i=1}^{n}(W_i * D_i + Fp) \tag{1}$$

$$Max \sum_{i=1}^{n}(K_i * D_i - Fp) \tag{2}$$

$$Fp = \frac{T_p - Pr}{T_p} * 100$$

$$Pr = D_p * \sum_{i=1}^{n}(P_i * D_i)$$

In which:

- i is the index of the analyst.
- Di is 1 if the analyst is present in the solution or 0 if it is not.
- n is the amount of analysts in the pool.
- W_i is the developer's remuneration.
- K_i is the developer's competence.
- P_i is the developer's productivity
- Fp is the factor of penalization.
- T_p is the size of the project (score).

– D_p is the number of working days available for carrying out the project.
– Pr is the total time productivity

Productivity is defined as the sum of the individual productivity of each selected analyst, multiplied by the number of working days. The factor of penalization reduces the values of the objective functions proportionally to how far the teams' productivity is from the target productivity (ProjectSize). Therefore, the key converges to solutions that meet the project size demands in the available time. This behavior differs from a linear programming, in which there are restrictions and the solutions that do not satisfy the conditions are eliminated. In the evolutionary algorithms studied and implemented in jMetal [9], the restrictions are selection criteria to find the most suitable for the next generation. Then, between two individuals, one that does present restrictions and another one that does not, the one who does not present restrictions will be chosen as apt for the next generation, even if this individual's objective functions are worse. Considering two individuals that present restrictions, the chosen one will be the person with the lower value of restriction. Thus, the restriction used in this experiment was:

$$Restriction = \begin{cases} 0, \text{if } Productivity \geq ProjectSize \\ ProjectSize - Productivity, \qquad \text{else} \end{cases}$$

4 Algorithms Utilized in the ATIMO Tool

The algorithms used for optimizing the teams are described as follows.

4.1 NSGA II

Algorithm 1: NSGA II

Generates the initial population randomly;
while *Performs the following loop by <Number of Generations> times* **do**

Duplicates the population by crossing it, selecting two individuals each time by binary tournament and mixing the genes according to the crossover selected. There is the possibility of mutation of the bit, with a configurable probability;
Ranks the population according to dominance;
Discards half the least apt population;
In case of draw, it randomly selects the individual;
end

4.2 SPEA2

Algorithm 2: SPEA2

Generates the initial Q population randomly;
Creates the empty P population;
while *Carries out the following loop by <Number of Generations> times* **do**

Calculates the fitness, objective functions, for the individuals of the
population;
Q receives the non dominating individuals of P + Q. If the number
is higher than the defined population, the least fitness ones are cut;
A binary tournament is performed in Q to select the parents who
will generate the new P population;
end
Ranks the populations and has as solution the best ranked (non dominating)
from Q population. In case of more than one solution, all of them are
presented;

4.3 MOCELL

Algorithm 3: MOCELL

Generates the initial Q population randomly;
Creates the empty P population;
while *Performs the following loop by <Number of Generations> times* **do**
  while *For each individual I in the population* **do**

Defines eight neighbors of this individual;
Picks a parent from the neighbors by binary tournament;
Picks a parent from the P population by binary tournament. If P
is empty, another neighbor is chosen;
Creates a new individual by crossing the parents;
Compares the new individual with I: adds the dominant in P and
assumes the actual position in the population, it is possible to be
the neighbors' choice;
  end
end
Ranks the P population and has as solution the best ranked, non
dominating, from the Q population. In case there is more than a solution, all
of them are presented.

4.4 Parameters of the Algorithms

The main parameters of each algorithm in jMetal are:

- Population Size.
  The initial population size, which is also the population size after each
  iteration.

– Number of generations.
  The amount of generations in the crossover and mutation cycle.
– Forms of representation:
  Binary. Every gene is represented by a bit that symbolizes the presence or absence of the analyst in the solution.
– Crossover
  For the binary form of representation, in JMetal, the following crossover methods can be applied:
  PointCrossOver: one position is randomly selected. In the copy of both parents, all of the positions after the score are changed and therefore results in the children.
  HUXCrossover (*Half Uniform Crossover*): in this approach half the different bits among the parents are changed. To do so it is necessary to calculate the amount of different bits. This number is divided by two and the result is the amount of different bits changed among the copies of the parents. Likewise are the results of the children.

5   The Experiment

In order to assess the ATIMO tool, developed for allocating resources, an experiment was conducted in a *software* company that uses the agile methodology - SCRUM. The experiment was carried out in one of the company's branches composed of 400 analysts including developers, testers, Scrum Masters, POs, among others, as resources. The company adopts 15-day Sprints and the release lasts for three months.

The main goal of the experiment was to compare the performance of the multi-objective optimizer algorithms NSGAII, SPEA2, and MOCell, selected from the literature, in the scope of allocation of agile teams for software development. All the algorithms utilized in this work were implemented by using the jMetal framework (Version 4.5.2)[1]. jMetal means meta-heuristic algorithms in Java and it is based on Java-oriented objects, aiming to facilitate the development of meta-heuristics to solve the *Multiobjective Optimization Problems* (MOPs). jMetal provides a set of classes that can be used as building blocks for multi-objective meta-heuristics; therefore promoting the reuse of the code, the algorithms share the same basic components such as the implementation of genetic operators and density estimators, enabling a fair comparison of different meta-heuristics for possible MOPs.

The first step was to identify the parameters to be considered when mapping the profile of the analysts. The developers were evaluated based on the following characteristics: Competences (knowledge, abilities, attitudes, culture); Remuneration, Productivity, and Assertiveness. The definition of these parameters was based on the concepts of Knowledge, Skills, and Attitudes (KSA) [5,11] and on the characteristics of agile teams [8]. Thus, it is possible to identify the number of human resources needed for the company software project, considering better qualifications and lower cost.

---

[1] http://jmetal.sourceforge.net/.

For Knowledge, sources of formal and informal knowledge were utilized in the performance of daily tasks. In this area, the developer's degree of knowledge concerning a range of topics were considered: technology, processes, product, project, among others. For the skills, the ones acquired from experience were taken into account. They were classified into categories: communication; collaboration; creativity; autonomy; emotional intelligence; curiosity; programming logic; strategic vision; leadership, and self-management. The attitudes were classified as follows: discipline; relationship; initiative; motivation; interest, and dedication; protagonism; commitment; mastery, and facilitator.

For each category the developer was evaluated in five levels: very low, low, average, high, very high. The data was obtained from the assessment carried out by the managers of the people belonging to the teams being studied along with the Scrum Masters, and the POs.

In question of culture, the score resulting from the **performance evaluation** used in the software company studied was considered as an organizational aspect that affects performance. The information was obtained through the automatic extraction of data from the company's human resources management software.

As parameters of remuneration in the developers' assessment, the data concerning salary was achieved from the tool that manages the payroll upon express authorization of the board in charge. However, for confidentiality purposes, the information was stratified in career levels and graduated from zero to 12.

The parameters productivity and assertiveness in the developers' evaluation were collected based on information by Squad and Sprint provided by Scrum Masters for the team in the Project Management Office (PMO).

Also, the mapping of the developers' profile was conducted aiming at mapping the profile of the professionals who work in development in the business segments chosen for the study. This mapping was made from the parameters, competences: technical knowledge, abilities, attitude, organizational culture, remuneration, productivity, and assertiveness in the projects handling. Data collection was made by the human resources managers and the POs. The salary of each analyst corresponding to the career level from zero to 12 was collected from payroll management system.

The PMO team provided information about the period of a year referring to the projects as well as the composition of each Squad, Sprint, the identification of the analysts, the amount of days in which the analyst took part in the Sprint, the number of points planned and delivered by the Squad. By adding the data by Sprint, and Squad, it is possible to calculate the average speed of the Squad in the Sprint, whereas adding the data by Squad, enables to calculate the average speed of that Squad.

5.1 Organization of the Project Scenarios for Carrying Out the Tests

The context of the experiment was explained to the two PMOs of the segments chosen for the study, who selected two real project scenarios that had already been performed in the company. For each scenario, the effort needed for running the project was raised, effort measured in score, the time they had to carry out the project, deadline for delivering to the customers, the technical and behavioural requirements necessary to the human resources taking part in the project. The score has already been normalized and each one of the three algorithms NSGAII, SPEA2, and MOCell were executed in their variants (with *Single Point Crossover* and *Hux Crossover*) 20 times, for the number of generations of 250 and the population ranging from: 100, 200, 300, ..., 800, 900, 1000; for the four scenarios. The data collected from the executions of the managers were added to this data. Afterwards, the experiment was complemented with data from the execution of NSGAII and SPEA2 with population ranging from 1100, 1200, ..., 1500, and the MOCell with the population varying from 1100, 1200, ..., 1900, 2000.

The scenarios they proposed are described as follows.

5.2   Test Scenario I

Building accounting indicators for the Core segment to be utilized in the BI solution. The context if from a project for building indicators, metrics, and reports for the Core segment. The project can be divided into three parts: **extractors** SQL queries in the databases *SQL Server* and *Oracle*; **modelling of Business Intelligence (BI):** modelling of the tables referring to the facts and dimensions, on the basis of granularity and the relevance of the data; ***Dashboards:*** building up metrics, reports, and graphs for viewing information. Desirable knowledge: average knowledge on Core, database, BI concepts, Gooddata platform. It requires a professional with good programming logic and that is able to work collaboratively, since it was necessary to obtain information from customers and from other areas. Given the project size of 3800 points and the maximum deadline of 480 working days.

5.3   Test Scenario II

Construction of predictive analytics solution. The context is part of a solution that can be developed in three parts: (1) Modelling of the solution according to their specific characteristics that will serve as an input for building the machine learning algorithm; (2) Modelling and setting of the MDM process as well as the data models for the process input and output data storage; (3) Creating the Web portal for displaying the prediction and management indicators.

Desirable knowledge: Angular JS, *Type Script*, HTML, CSS, average knowledge of Core, platform of artificial intelligence ownership, database. It requires a professional with good programming logic, initiative, self-taught, easy to get along with, and self motivated. Because this is an innovative project, it demands a great deal of R&D. This project has a 1.950 points size and the maximum deadline is 360 working days.

5.4   Test Scenario III

The context of the project is the evolution of the sales portal, in this case the need for improvement was identified concerning enhancing processes and interface changes. The desirable knowledge is: PHP, Mobile, WEB, knowledge aboutUser Experience (UX), Core product knowledge. In this scenario the project size is 500 points and the deadline is 120 working days.

5.5   Test Scenario IV

The context is a migration project for the Core product integration with the Backoffice, allowing for an integration framework with the clipping model, in which the financial solution is in charge of managing the Core solution receivables. Desirable knowledge is: Backoffice, having already taken part of a project of integration migration in the same scope, knowledge about the involved framework, deep knowledge on the current integration architecture, knowledge of architecture, seniority, pro-activity, knowledge about the financial solution. The project size is 300 points and the deadline is 60 working days.

5.6   Conducting the Experiments

A group of 10 *Scrum Masters* from segments selected for the study were invited for the performance of the experiment. A step-by-step for carrying out the experiment was elaborated. Initially, the participants were told the context of the research and the goals of the experiment. The project scenarios to be simulated were presented and the project parameters were defined by the PMO of the segment in question. With this information, the group was invited to go over all the information and validate it. When the group arrived at a consensus about the project parameters, the simulation started. The PMO attended this meeting to clarify the Scrum Masters' doubts.

Each participant had as objective to determine the number of analysts required for the project as well as choosing the most suitable analysts for the project scenarios studied, taking into consideration the most competent analysts, with enough productivity to meet the deadline requested for delivery and that had the lower cost, lower salary level. The participants were oriented as of the use of the tool to support the team selection. From the scenarios presented, each participant individually carried out the simulation picking a team for each project scenario presented. The PMO who elaborated the scenario also carried out the simulation previously, but the data was not considered in the results, only to assess the adequacy of the experiment. 20 simulations were carried out: four scenarios and five people per scenario. The data obtained from each simulation was recorded in a log for subsequent analysis. After the manual simulation, the optimizer algorithms were executed and the results were also recorded in the log.

In the experiment, the participants used the ATIMO to compose the team according to the project scenarios described. First, they informed the overall resources of the project such as the size of team, working days, and the skills required for the project, such as: technologies, database, tools, and so on. The Fig. 1 shows the screen[2] of ATIMO for this task. Next, they selected the developer knowledge with the corresponding weight for the knowledge required for the project. Figure 2 presents the ATIMOS screen for this task. After, ATIMO shows the available developers with respective scores for each category of competence, productivity, and remuneration. So, the participants selected the developer that best met the project requirements. experiment used this simulation to compare

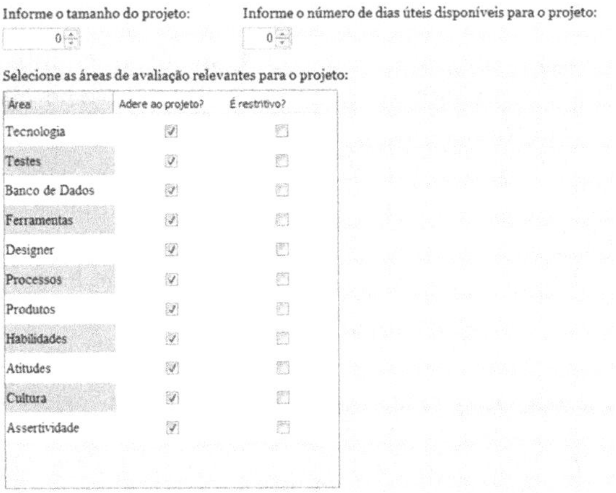

Source: research data.

Fig. 1. Selection of skills required for the project

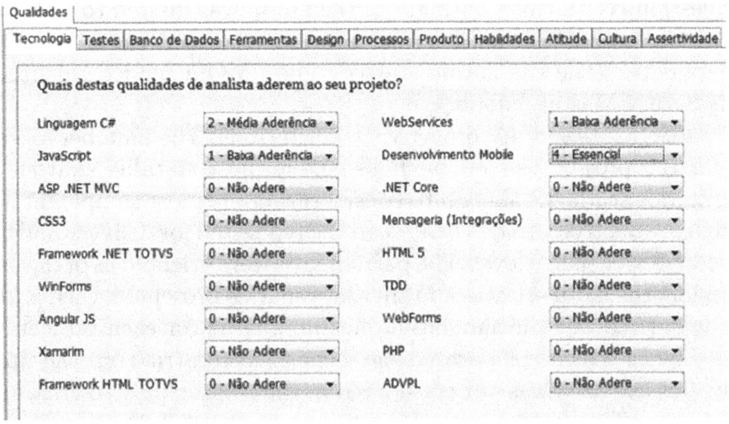

Source: research data.

Fig. 2. Selection of developer knowledge

---

[2] The ATIMO's labels are in Portuguese because the experiment was applied in a Brazilian software company.

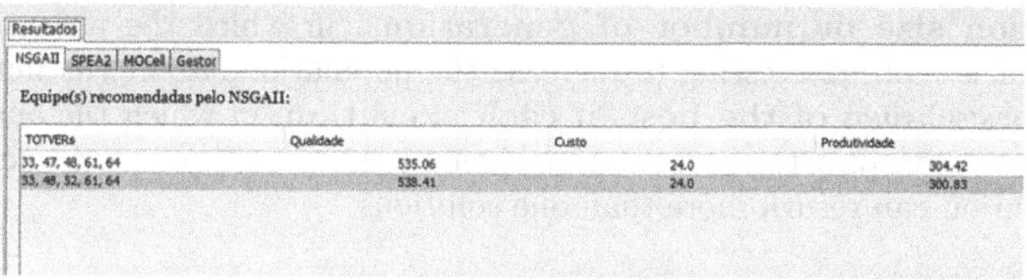

Source: research data.

Fig. 3. Selection of developer knowledge

with the result presented by the optimization algorithms. Figure 3 presents the results of the experiment where each tab represents the results suggested by the algorithms and the participant's choice.

The main parameters of each algorithm in jMetal are: population size, the number of generations; the amount of generations in the crossover and mutation cycle and every gene is represented by a bit. For the binary form of representation in JMetal, the following *crossover* methods can be utilized: *PointCrossOver*: only one position is randomly selected. When copying both parents, all the positions after the point are changed and, thus, they the children are results. *HUX-Crossover (Half Uniform Crossover)*: in this approach, half the different bits among the parents are changed. Thus, it is necessary to calculate the amount of different bits. This number is divided by two and the resulting number is the amount of different bits changed among the copies of the parents. Likewise are the results of the children.

In the execution of the algorithms throughout the experiment, the maximum parameters for generations were utilized, population size, size of variables set, crossover probability, mutation probability. Given that, the maximum of generations and the population size were parameterized according to each scenario, the size of the variables set was the number of analysts available, the probability of crossover was 90% and the probability of mutation was 50% out of the number of analysts available.

In this study, the parameters were defined based on similar works carried out identified in the literature that had consistent results. The choice of the crossover and mutation parameters based on the works presented in [6, 14–16, 18]. In the simulation, the parameters maximum number of generations and the population size varied according to the experiment of the study. The size of variables set is the same as of the number of analysts available for forming the team, since each gene represents the presence or absence of the analyst in the solution. In Sect. 6, the results obtained with this methodology are presented.

Section 6 presents the results of the **variation of the population size**, in which the number of generations is fixed in 250 and the population size varies for the studied algorithms; **variation of the number of generations**, in which the population size is fixed and the number of generation varies; **measuring the performance of the algorithms**, in which the execution is measured,

population size or number of generations, in which the analysis is on whether it is more interesting to increase the population size or the number of generations; **choice of the best of each execution**, in which the analysis is made considering only the best solution given by the algorithm in each execution: one execution can return more than one solutions.

6   Results and Discussion

In order to present the performance of algorithms used in ATIMO tool, in this section, it is possible to see in Tables 1, 2, 3, and 4 the comparisons of the average results presented for the algorithms configured with the bigger population, ordered by the value of **quality** (the number of competence score) divided by the **cost**, for the four scenarios of the experiment:

When comparing the quality and cost of the best algorithm regarding the managers, it is noticeable the delivery of, in average, 13,44% (MOCell), 13,03% (SPEA2), 60,11% (NSGAII), and 33,94% (NSGAII) more quality and cost than the average managers, for the scenarios I, II, III, and IV, respectively.

Table 1. Scenario I varying the population size

Algorithm	Quality/cost	Quality	Cost	Productivity
MOCELL_Binary	10.782493	572.023599	54.561947	3818.306254
SPEA2_Binary	10.631735	617.750000	58.142857	3800.862857
NSGAII_Binary	10.126990	662.727273	65.515152	3853.703030
Manager	9.502051	613.400000	65.400000	3903.954000
NSGAII_Binary_HUXCrossover	8.027127	1015.446429	126.982143	7055.401786
MOCELL_Binary_HUXCrossover	7.900434	991.764706	125.588235	7005.171176
SPEA2_Binary_HUXCrossover	7.872259	1027.563636	130.527273	7221.774182

Table 2. Scenario II varying the population size

Algorithm	Quality/cost	Quality	Cost	Productivity
SPEA2_Binary	11.884401	429.600000	36.200000	1944.450400
NSGAII_Binary	11.631291	443.764706	38.205882	1945.612824
MOCELL_Binary	11.147568	405.767760	37.401639	1942.472732
Manager	10.518975	458.400000	44.000000	2115.604000
NSGAII_Binary_HUXCrossover	7.543934	952.125000	126.200000	5348.226750
MOCELL_Binary_HUXCrossover	7.456709	886.485714	118.971429	5104.342857
SPEA2_Binary_HUXCrossover	7.443610	846.000000	114.029412	4836.977647

Table 3. Scenario III varying the population size

Algorithm	Quality/cost	Quality	Cost	Productivity
NSGAII_Binary	15.759171	395.351351	25.162162	301.431892
SPEA2_Binary	15.386973	405.913043	26.434783	301.546957
MOCELL_Binary	13.762170	380.288820	28.673913	300.832919
Manager	9.842172	432.200000	44.600000	301.156000
NSGAII_Binary_HUXCrossover	7.741285	917.138889	118.722222	866.447778
SPEA2_Binary_HUXCrossover	7.293457	885.250000	121.468750	860.554375
MOCELL_Binary_HUXCrossover	7.201363	866.833333	120.666667	856.605333

Table 4. Scenario IV varying the population size

Algorithm	Quality/cost	Quality	Cost	Productivity
SPEA2_Binary	6.404832	136.958333	21.416667	484.972917
NSGAII_Binary	6.214730	152.521739	24.652174	485.479783
MOCELL_Binary	5.354286	124.527344	23.738281	489.093242
Manager	4.781672	172.600000	36.800000	576.936000
SPEA2_Binary_HUXCrossover	2.550990	307.440000	120.200000	1722.890000
NSGAII_Binary_HUXCrossover	2.504675	282.185185	112.703704	1653.634074
MOCELL_Binary_HUXCrossover	2.500024	300.312500	120.375000	1770.900625

Table 5. Better quality and cost of each scenario

Scenario	Algorithm	Productivity	Quality/cost
I	MOCell	3846,1	15,0625
II	MOCell	1806,52	16,2105
III	MOCell	300,64	18,2941
IV	MOCell	482,17	7,1428

Source: research data.

As it can be seen from Tables 1, 2, 3, and 4, the quality and cost of the algorithms executed with *Hux Crossover* were below the ones executed with *Single Point Crossover* in all scenarios. Therefore, the focus will be only on the results obtained from the *Single Point Crossover* algorithms. Besides that, it is interesting to observe that, although MOCell has average results close to the compared algorithms, it presents expressive results. Table 5, shows the results with best quality and cost of each scenario and the respective algorithm. In all the scenarios, MOCell was the algorithm that presented the best solution. Respectively, 58,49%, 54,11%, 85,88%, and 49,38% higher than the average result of the managers. These results were higher than the average of the best algorithm of the scenario.

An additional test was carried out. By setting the population size to 250 and varying the number of generations from 100 to 1.000: in scenario I, the best algorithm was in average 16,28% (MOCell) better than the average result of the managers. It was also noticed an improvement in MOCell rather than in the compared algorithms when the number of generations increases. In scenarios II, III, and IV, the best algorithm delivered 14,64% (SPEA2), 60,73% (NSGAII), and 31,21% (SPEA2) more quality/cost than the average managers, respectively. Thus, the evolution of the quality and cost results in each scenario varying the number of generations was similar to the previously presented ones varying the population size, regarding which algorithm performed best.

All the algorithms were executed in a computer with the following setting: Intel Core i5-7200U processor CPU 2.50 GHz 2.71 GHz, RAM memory of 16 GB executed in Windows 64 bits. The execution time spent with MOCell with a population of 2.000 is approximately the same spent on NSGAII and SPEA2 with a population of 600 and 500, respectively.

In all of the scenarios the percentage average improvement between 100 and 1.000 of population was compared setting the number of generations to 250 with the percentage average improvement between 100 and 1.000 generations, setting the population size in 250. In all scenarios the improvement was higher for MOCell, compared with the other two algorithms. This proves that MOCell is greedier by population size as well as by number of generations bigger than the compared algorithms. In compensation, NSGAII was the least greedy. As such, it is noticeable the advantage of investing in population instead of number of generations. However, the increase in population in the algorithms SPEA2 and NSGAII reflects the quadratic increase in the execution time, while the increase in the number of generations is linear. Therefore, it makes sense to conclude the predilection for increasing the number of generations in SPEA2 an NSGAII instead of the population size and the inverse for MOCell.

In this study, each one of the 20 executions was numbered so that each algorithm could return more than one solution. The solutions were filtered in order to keep only the best result of each execution, the one with greater quality and cost value. This procedure has special effect in MOCell, which returns many solutions, as its objective is also to provide a bigger and better sample of the Pareto front [2]. Thus, by choosing the best solution of each execution, better quality and cost for each scenario, MOCell was in average, superior to the compared algorithms in the three first scenarios and being statistically equivalent in each execution.

By filtering the solutions in order to select the best one from each execution, through the best quality and cost, MOCell presented superior average in the three first scenarios and a similar result compared to the compared algorithms in the fourth scenario. It is a characteristic of the algorithm the high variance, since one of its objectives is to represent well the Pareto front [2]. In practical terms, interesting results could be presented if the algorithm were executed a few times and the best solutions were collected, as in all the scenarios the best solution derived from this algorithm.

In addition to that, in the same work [2], the improvement of MOCell was noticed by using a *feedback* approach of the non dominating population archived, randomly replacing the population of the next iteration. This enhancement was not contemplated in this work given that in the JMetal version adopted it was not implemented in MOCell, but the other versions of the algorithm, names as sMOCell and aMOCell, which were not tested in this study. Then, there is still the possibility of the algorithm presenting better results than the ones observed here.

Finally, based on the data verified for this scenario, the utilization of MOCell with a population of 2.000 and by selecting the best solution from each execution is highlighted. In case it is inserted in a scope in which it is possible to await the result, it is also possible to collect the best solutions from many executions, considering that these are better than the average, but presented fewer times, regarding the total amount of executions.

The average results of managers were calculated and compared with results of the ATIMO. With 75% of confidence, the algorithms implemented in ATIMO outperformed the managers'. Therefore, we can confirm that ATIMO can be used as a tool to put together agile teams in software development companies. However, in the moment this paper was being written, the tool was still in the testing phase to improve the results quality and usability, so it is not yet available outside the company.

7   Threats to the Validity of Research

This study evaluated optimization algorithms in order to put agile teams together in software projects. However, threats to validity of the research may be considered. First, in the experiment, the parameters were not tuned. Thus, these parameters may affect the comparison. To avoid these problems, the setup parameters highlighted in the literature were used. Also, the indicators hypervolume, coverage, and Inverted Generational Distance (IGD) were not evaluated. In order to compensate, an empirical approach was used based on the allocation of teams by managers.

The experiment was applied to one company and in a few projects. In order to improve the tool, the intention is to expand the use of the tool to other projects and other companies.

8   Conclusion

The objective of this research was to assess the performance of optimization techniques applied to the allocation of agile teams in software development. With this purpose, the ATIMO tool was developed, allowing for the managers to use three optimizer algorithms NSGAII, SPEA2, and MOCell. To evaluate the tool, an experiment was carried out in a software development company that adopts the agile methodology in its projects. Four real company scenarios were tested in the experiment, in which the tested algorithms proved adherent to the problem posed. The algorithms SPEA2 and NSGAII presented similar results and NSGAII is less greedier, for this reason, it reaches a saturation point with less population than SPEA2, besides having a better computational performance. Therefore, the use of NSGAII for the studied cases is recommended, even if MOCell had expressive results, although with a bigger population. Future research can invest in assessing the performance of MOCell by using the feedback approach of the non dominating population archived, randomly replacing the population of the next iteration. Another opportunity for future research would be to invest in the study of the algorithms configuration parameters evaluating the approach of automation of a set of parameters to be modified during its execution and analysis of the results achieved.

References

1. Adenso-Díaz, B., Gonzalez-Torre, P., Garcia, V.: A capacity management model in service industries. Int. J. Serv. Ind. Manag. **13**(3), 286–302 (2002)
2. Nebro, A.J., Durillo, J.J., Luna, F., Dorronsoro, B., Alba, E.: MOCell: a cellular genetic algorithm for multiobjective optimization. Int. J. Intell. Syst. **24**, 726–746 (2009). https://doi.org/10.1002/int.20358
3. Barreto, A., de Oliveira Barros, M., Werner, C.M.L.: Staffing a software project: a constraint satisfaction and optimization-based approach. Comput. Oper. Res. **35**(10), 3073–3089 (2008). https://doi.org/10.1016/j.cor.2007.01.010
4. Bibi, N., Ahsan, A., Anwar, Z.: Project resource allocation optimization using search based software engineering - a framework. In: Proceedings of the 9th International Conference on Digital Information Management (ICDIM 2014), Phitsanulok, Thailand, pp. 226–229. IEEE, 29 September–1 October 2014. https://doi.org/10.1109/ICDIM.2014.6991431
5. Britto, R., Neto, P.S., Rabelo, R., Ayala, W., Soares, T.: A hybrid approach to solve the agile team allocation problem. In: Proceedings of IEEE Congress on Evolutionary Computation (CEC 2012), Brisbane, Australia, pp. 1–8, 10–15 June 2012. IEEE (2012). https://doi.org/10.1109/CEC.2012.6252999
6. Cervantes, J., Stephens, C.R.: Optimal mutation rates for genetic search. In: Proceedings of the 8th Annual Conference on Genetic and Evolutionary Computation, pp. 1313–1320. ACM (2006)
7. Connor, A.M., Shah, A.: Resource allocation using metaheuristic search. In: Proceedings of the 4th International Conference on Computer Science and Information Technology (CCSIT 2014), Sydney, Australia, 21–22 February 2014. https://doi.org/10.5121/csit.2014.4230
8. Coram, M., Bohner, S.: The impact of agile methods on software project management. In: 12th IEEE International Conference and Workshops on the Engineering of Computer-Based Systems, ECBS 2005, pp. 363–370. IEEE (2005)
9. Durillo, J.J., Nebro, A.J.: jMetal: a Java framework for multi-objective optimization. Adv. Eng. Softw. **42**, 760–771 (2011). https://doi.org/10.1016/j.advengsoft.2011.05.014. http://www.sciencedirect.com/science/article/pii/S0965997811001219
10. Fagerholm, F., Ikonen, M., Kettunen, P., Münch, J., Roto, V., Abrahamsson, P.: Performance alignment work: how software developers experience the continuous adaptation of team performance in lean and agile environments. Inf. Softw. Technol. **64**, 132–147 (2015)

11. Gangani, N., McLean, G.N., Braden, R.A.: A competency-based human resource development strategy. Perform. Improv. Q. **19**(1), 127–139 (2006)

12. Hoda, R., Noble, J., Marshall, S.: Organizing self-organizing teams. In: 2010 ACM/IEEE 32nd International Conference on Software Engineering, vol. 1, pp. 285–294. IEEE (2010)

13. Ingold, D., Boehm, B., Koolmanojwong, S.: A model for estimating agile project process and schedule acceleration. In: Proceedings of the 2013 International Conference on Software and System Process, pp. 29–35. ACM (2013)

14. Khalil, E., Assaf, M., Sayyad, A.S.: Human resource optimization for bug fixing: balancing short-term and long-term objectives. In: Menzies, T., Petke, J. (eds.) SSBSE 2017. LNCS, vol. 10452, pp. 124–129. Springer, Cham (2017). https://doi.org/10.1007/978-3-319-66299-2_9

15. Ochoa, G.: Setting the mutation rate: scope and limitations of the 1/l heuristic. In: Proceedings of the 4th Annual Conference on Genetic and Evolutionary Computation, pp. 495–502. Morgan Kaufmann Publishers Inc. (2002)

16. del Sagrado, J., del Aguila, I.M., Orellana, F.J.: Multi-objective ant colony optimization for requirements selection. Empir. Softw. Eng. **20**(3), 577–610 (2015)

17. Sayyad, A.S., Ammar, H.: Pareto-optimal search-based software engineering (POS-BSE): a literature survey. In: 2013 2nd International Workshop on Realizing Artificial Intelligence Synergies in Software Engineering (RAISE), pp. 21–27, May 2013. https://doi.org/10.1109/RAISE.2013.6615200

18. Wen, F., Lin, C.M.: Multistage human resource allocation for software development by multiobjective genetic algorithm. Open Appl. Math. J. **2**, 95–103 (2008). http://www.bentham.org/open/toamj/articles/V002/95TOAMJ.pdf

A Survey on Agile Practices
and Challenges of a Global Software
Development Team

Tatiane Lautert$^{(\boxtimes)}$ ⓘ, Adolfo Gustavo Serra Seca Neto ⓘ,
and Nádia P. Kozievitch ⓘ

Universidade Tecnológica Federal do Parana (UTFPR), Curitiba, Brazil
tatianelautert@alunos.utfpr.edu.br, {adolfo,nadiap}@utfpr.edu.br

Abstract. The Agile Manifesto describes that the most efficient and
effective method of conveying information to and within a development team is through face-to-face conversation. However that is not
always possible when teams are working in a Global Software Development (GSD) environment. Based on this scenario, this study presents
an exploratory data analysis using survey results to explore agile practices and challenges of a global software development team that uses
Scaled Agile Framework (SAFe), which is designed for the need of larger
organizations. The goal of this study is to understand the team's level
of knowledge in some agile practices and which types of communication are usually prioritized. As in GSD environments team members are
geographically spread across multiple regions and time zones, we aim
to identify challenges this environment can present. As a result of this
exploratory analysis, it has been identified that communication is one
of main challenges in GSD environment and that phone calls are considered to be the most efficient type of communication. Additionally, we
have also identified that professionals have different levels of confidence
in Agile practices and concluded that knowledge transfers among the
professionals could help those team members that are not confident in
some agile practices to increase their overall confidence and knowledge.

Keywords: Agile methodologies · Survey · Global Software
Development · SAFe

1 Introduction

Agile software development is based on a set of 4 values and 12 principles
described in the Agile Manifesto[1]. It was written in 2001 by a group of 17
practitioners interested in finding better ways of developing software that is
centered on individuals but also is able to respond to rapid changes. Agile Software development can be described as a lightweight methodology as opposed

---

[1] https://agilemanifesto.org/, last accessed 12 May 2019.

© Springer Nature Switzerland AG 2019
P. Meirelles et al. (Eds.): WBMA 2019, CCIS 1106, pp. 128–143, 2019.
https://doi.org/10.1007/978-3-030-36701-5_11

to heavyweight traditional software engineering processes. One of the principles of the Agile Manifesto describes that the most efficient and effective method of conveying information to and within a development team is through face-to-face conversation, however that is not always possible when teams are working in a Global Software Development (GSD) environment.

According to Herbsleb and Moitra [1], software has become a crucial component for almost every business in recent years and developing software or implementing changes to software that responds to markets' demands is a competitive advantage, vital for business success. Over the recent decades many organizations began to experiment with remotely located software development facilities and with outsourcing, seeking lower costs and skilled resources. The authors highlight that potential benefits of GSD should not be neglected, however a number of problems are also identified and communication is one of them. In order to respond to these rapid market demands, the IT industry has been adopting Agile software development practices and frameworks such as Scrum, Extreme Programming (XP), Lean, Crystal, Dynamic Systems Development Method (DSDM), Feature Driven Development (FDD), and others.

These frameworks or methods provide guidelines which are usually tailored for small teams and serve well for enabling the execution of their development, coordination and communication tasks. However, these methods by themselves do not scale to the need of larger organizations where hundreds of professionals are involved in the development of large and complex solutions [2]. In that scenario, during recent years, several frameworks for scaling agile have been created including Scaled Agile Framework (SAFe), Large-scale Scrum (LeSS) and Disciplined Agile Delivery (DAD) as cited by Paasivaara [3].

Scaled Agile Framework (SAFe)[2] was created by Dean Leffingwell and its latest version is SAFe 4.6. It is composed of 4 different configurations, being them: Essential SAFe, Portfolio SAFe, Large Solution SAFe and Full SAFe. Each of these configurations have a set of organization levels (Portfolio, Large Solution, Program and Team) and each level contains details and guidelines about roles, activities, events, and processes applicable to each level. At the Program Level, SAFe uses the concept of the Agile Release Train (ART) which can be described as a virtual organization composed of around 50 to 125 people that are aligned to a business mission and they work together to plan, commit, develop and deploy the solutions. In SAFe's website there is an interactive picture which contains links that take to web pages with more details on each role, processes, activities, and others that are part of the framework[3].

In this study, a survey was conducted with a GSD team of a large financial services organization that uses SAFe. The team is composed of about 170 professionals that form two Agile Release Trains (ARTs). These professionals are spread across multiple locations where majority of them are based in the United States, Brazil and India. The members of each of these Scrum teams can be located in the same region or sometimes there could be different location

---

[2] https://www.scaledagileframework.com, last accessed 12 May 2019.

[3] https://www.scaledagileframework.com/, last accessed 10-Jun-2019.

arrangements as well. Typically, Product Owners, Development Managers, Business Analysts and Program related roles are based in the US while Developers, System Analysts and Technical Leads are based in Brazil or India but that is not a fixed location arrangement.

The objective of this survey is to understand the level of knowledge of some agile practices by these professionals, which types of communication are usually prioritized and what challenges GSD environments can present. Additionally, the aim is to answer the following research question:

[Q1] Professionals with more experience in agile methodologies prioritize synchronous or asynchronous communication?

The data was collected through this survey and in this study an exploratory data analysis is presented.

2   Related Work

As highlighted by Hossain et al. [6] there is a growing interest in applying agile practices in Global Software Development (GSD) projects. In this paper the authors conduct a systematic literature review of the primary studies that report using Scrum practices in GSD environment and the objective of their study was to identify various challenging factors that restrict the use of Scrum practices in projects that are globally distributed. One of their conclusions is that Scrum practices need to be extended or modified in order to support globally distributed software development teams.

Fitriani et al. [5] also conducted a systematic literature review and found that there are 30 challenges in implementing Agile Software Development. Among these 30 challenges, the authors concluded that the most significant challenges are team management and distributed team, followed by requirement prioritization, documentation, changing and over-scoping requirement, organization, process, and progress monitoring and feedback.

Other studies that investigate Agile practices and challenges are for example Salinas et al. [4] and Nazir et al. [7]. Both papers describe surveys. In the first paper the authors focus on the Paraguayan software community and how this community is adopting agile methods. They present initial concerns and barriers of implementation of agile methods in software development companies in Paraguay. In the second paper, the authors focus on the investigation of the extent of agile practices adoption in regards to the Indian IT Industry concluding that agile practices affect the cost and increase the productivity.

Similarly, in this research a survey is conducted in order to identify Agile practices and challenges. However the focus of this work is on distributed teams that work on a Global Software Development environment.

3   Method

The survey was conducted during the team's Innovation and Planning Iteration (IP), which is an event defined in SAFe's framework that is dedicated for

Product Increment events, innovation activities, training and others. The exact period was from 11/April/2019 to 24/April/2019. During this period the survey was created using Microsoft Forms[4] and a link to the survey was provided by email to the team members. The survey remained open for 4 days and after that preliminary results were presented to the team during the IP Iteration Demo meeting.

The survey was composed of 18 questions, of which 17 were closed-ended questions and 1 was an open-ended question. Table 1 shows details about the types of questions in the survey.

The data was then exported to Excel format, transformed as needed and imported into Python[5] analysis library, Pandas[6], so that data could be manipulated as needed and visual graphs could be generated accordingly. Other Python libraries were also used to generate different types of graphs.

We received 32 responses, which represent around 19% of the population to whom the survey was sent to. Out of these 32 responses, 18 respondents answered the open-ended question which was the only question for which the answer was not mandatory among the 18 survey questions.

Table 1. Types of questions in the survey.

Question type	Allowed multiple answers	Answer required	Likert	N. of statements in Likert	N. of options in Likert	Total by type
Open-ended	NA	No	No	NA	NA	1
Close-ended	Yes	Yes	No	N/A	N/A	3
Close-ended	No	Yes	No	N/A	N/A	8
Close-ended	No	Yes	Yes	10	5	1
Close-ended	No	Yes	Yes	1	5	5
Total						18

Please note that the full list of the survey questions is in the appendix section.

4   Results

In this section, the results of each survey question is presented. The first question was to identify the role of the respondents. Since this survey was anonymous, those roles that have only one or two professionals were not explicitly listed, hence these are aggregated as 'Others'. As shown in Fig. 1 the majority of the respondents were developers (14), followed by Quality Assurance - Tester (5), Technical Lead and Software Analyst (4 each), Development Manager and Scrum Master (2 each) and Other (1). No Architects and no Product Owners responded to the survey.

---

[4] https://forms.office.com, last accessed 18-May-2019.
[5] https://www.python.org/, last accessed 18-May-2019.
[6] https://pandas.pydata.org/, last accessed 18-May-2019.

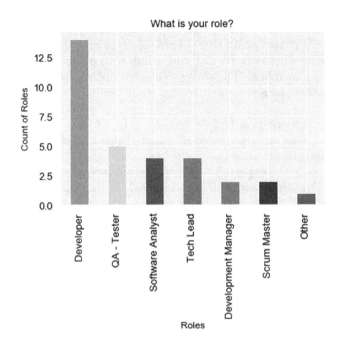

Fig. 1. Q1 - Roles distribution.

Question 2 was to identify how many years of experience in Agile Software Development the respondents have. As shown in Fig. 2, it was found that 12 professionals have from 1 to 3 years of experience, 12 have 4 to 7 years of experience, 7 have more than 8 years of experience and 1 respondent has less than 1 year of experience.

In question 3, professionals were asked to select all Agile Methodologies they have experience with. In Fig. 3 it is possible to see that Scrum is the most known framework by these professionals, followed by SAFe, which seems appropriate given the fact that SAFe is the framework used by the company as explained previously.

In question 4, participants were asked if they had already taken any training on any Agile methodology and it was found that 75% of the participants had already taken training on Agile methodology while 25% have not taken any training. Based on this result, the company could take actions to provide training courses to those who have not taken any training yet.

Question 5 presented a Likert scale question, in which participants were asked to assess their familiarity with Agile methodologies in a scale of extremely familiarized, very familiarized, familiarized, not so familiarized or not familiarized at all. Figure 4 shows the results of their own assessment on this topic. In general, most participants feel they are either very familiarized or familiarized with Agile methodologies.

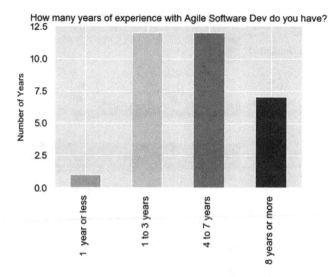

Fig. 2. Q2 - Years of experience in Agile Methodology.

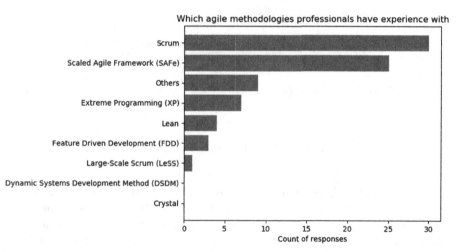

Fig. 3. Q3 - Agile Methodologies which professionals had experience with.

Question 6 presents another Likert scale question, but this time participants were asked to assess their familiarity with SAFe. The results show that their familiarity decreased when compared to the previous question which was more generic as opposed to a specific framework as in question 6. However it is possible to see that most participants, 69% in total feel they are familiarized with SAFe (Fig. 5).

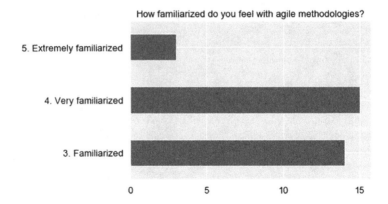

Fig. 4. Q5 - Familiarity with Agile Methodologies.

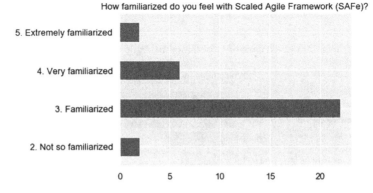

Fig. 5. Q4 - Familiarity with SAFe.

In question 7, 10 different Agile practices and terms were selected and participants were asked to scale their confidence level on each of the selected practices and terms. Figure 6 shows the results in percentages per level of confidence. It is possible to see that a representative percentage of participants are not confident with a few practices, for example: 22% of the participants are not confident and 6% are not confident at all with Behaviour Driven Development practice, 25% are not confident and 3% are not confident at all with Test Driven Development practice, 22% are not confident and 6% are not confident at all with Pair Programming practice, 25% are not confident and 6% are not confident at all with Refactoring. With these results is it also possible to see that there are participants that feel extremely confident with some of these practice, perhaps that can indicate that knowledge transfer among the team members can increase the level of confidence to those who do not feel confident.

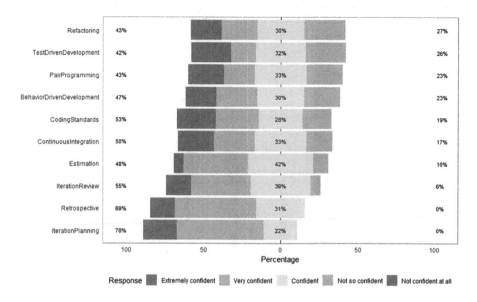

Fig. 6. Q7 - Confidence with Agile practices or terms.

Question 8 to 12 are all related to types of communication used by the participants and their evaluation of efficiency to some of these communication types. Figure 7 shows that e-mails and Skype chats are the types of communication most prioritized by these professionals, followed by 'Face-to-face, whenever possible' (22) and phone calls (19). 27 out of 32 participants selected email and Skype chats are their most prioritized type of communication. Only 1 participant selected video calls.

Figure 8 shows the biggest impediments for not communicating more via phone, face-to-face or via video calls. Time-zone constraints and agenda conflicts are the main causes, representing a total of 35% each.

Figure 9 shows how participants evaluate the efficiency of communication via e-mail, Skype chat and phone calls. It is possible to see that phone calls are considered the most efficient type of communication, followed by Skype chat and emails being the least efficient.

In question 13, participants were asked to respond how often they discuss project related items with the Product Owners (POs) or request feedback on features or stories, based on the fact that the 4th Agile principal, described in the Agile Manifesto says: 'Business people and developers must work together daily throughout the project'. Only 25% of the participants responded that they have daily communication with the Product Owner, 47% responded 'Once or twice per iteration', 19% responded 'Every other iteration' and 9% only during the Product Increment planning, which occurs every 3 months (Fig. 10).

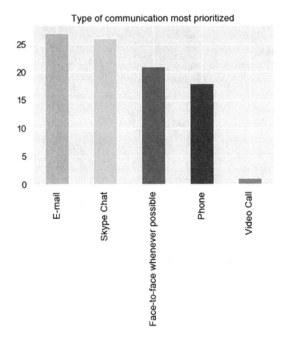

Fig. 7. Q8 - Types of communication prioritized.

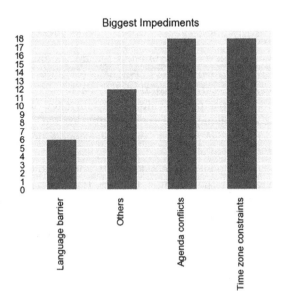

Fig. 8. Q9 - Impediments for not having more phone, face-to-face or video calls.

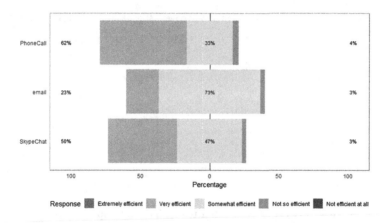

Fig. 9. Q10 - Evaluation of communication efficiency per type.

Fig. 10. Q13 - How often teams discuss project items with PO or request feedback.

Questions 14 and 15 were related to retrospective meetings. The results show that 97% of the respondents have a retrospective meeting once per iteration and 91% said that retrospective meetings are resulting in actionable items to bring improvements, which is aligned with Agile principle 12 which says: 'At regular intervals, the team reflects on how to become more effective, then tunes and adjusts its behavior accordingly' (Figs. 11 and 12).

In question 16, participants were asked if and how they were planning their capacity according to the team's velocity. The team's velocity in the company is measured in story points and to track team's capacity, a sum of story points that each team each team member can delivery for each iteration is made. Story point estimation is used to size stories, typically through pointing poker technique. The results show that 44% of the respondents said their team's capacity is usually at 100% and 41% are usually at 80% (Fig. 13).

The last closed-ended question was related to how these professionals would control/track budget in an Agile project. The first SAFe principle is 'Take an economic view' and as per SAFe's guidelines, economics should inform and drive

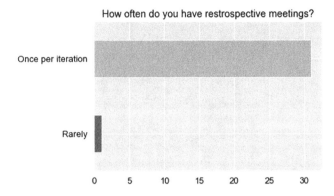

Fig. 11. Q14 - How often teams have retrospectives.

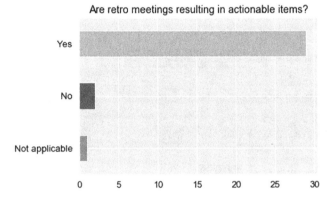

Fig. 12. Q15 - Are retrospectives resulting in actions/improvements?

decisions at all levels, from Portfolio to Development Teams, therefore it is important that every team member has an idea of how to control budgets in an Agile project. Figure 14 shows that 63% of the respondents were not sure how to control budget, 22% responded that it would be 'Through planned and defined budget to cover the life cycle of the project', 9% responded 'Through incremental budget aligned in each phase' and 6% responded 'Through initial budget to cover MVP and the remaining budget to be discussed depending on MVP results'.

The last question was an open-ended question. Participants were asked what is/are the main challenge(s) of running an Agile development project with remote teams. Since this was an open-ended question, it was decided to generated a World Cloud graph, which is a visual representation of text data and the importance of each word is represented its size in the graph and based on the number of times these words were mentioned on the text data. In Fig. 15 it becomes clear that communication is considered one of the main challenges raised by the participants.

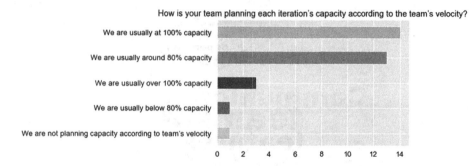

Fig. 13. Q16 - Are teams planning capacity based on velocity?

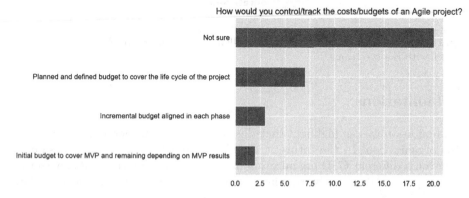

Fig. 14. Q17 - How teams believe budget are controlled in Agile projects.

Regarding the research question raised in this study, which aimed to identify whether professionals with more experience in agile methodologies prioritize synchronous or asynchronous communication, Fig. 16 shows a slightly higher correlation between years of experience and face-to-face communication (0.5), followed by email (0.46) and video call (0.45) communications if compared to other types of communication, although there is no strong correlation with any specific type of communication. There is strong correlation between types of communication prioritized, for example those who tend to prioritize Skype chat would also prioritize e-mail (0.99), those who tend to prioritize face-to-face communication would also prioritize phone calls (0.99).

Fig. 15. Q18 - Word cloud with main challenges in running an Agile development project with remote teams.

5   Limitations

As a limitation we can highlight that this survey has been conducted on a single GSD organization. In the future it would be interesting to conduct a similar survey on a different GSD organization in order to compare the results with the present study. Additionally, the data presented in this study represent around

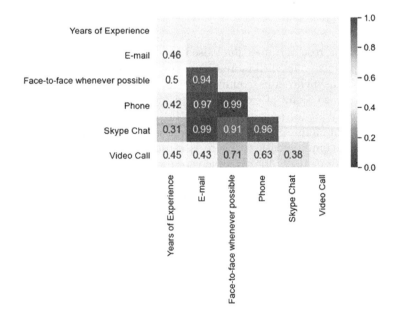

Fig. 16. Years of experience correlation with types of communication.

19% of the population to whom the survey was sent to. If more responses had been collected the results of this study would be richer. Also, the analysis of the open-ended question could be enriched by looking at individual responses and conducting follow-up interviews with team members in an attempt to address the challenges that have been reported.

6   Conclusion

With the results of this study, it is clear that communication is one of the main challenges in running Agile projects in Global Software Development. Also, it was possible to confirm that there is no strong correlation between years of experience in Agile Software Development with types of communication prioritized. Results also showed that phone calls are considered to be the most efficient type of communication in Global Software Development environment. Additionally, it was possible to see that professionals have different levels of confidence in Agile practices, knowledge transfers among the professionals could help those team members that are not confident in some agile practices to increase their overall confidence and knowledge.

A   Appendices

A.1   Agile Survey

Objective: The objective of this survey is to assess the level of knowledge in agile practices of the professionals and how communication barriers are overcome.

1. What is your role?
   Options: Developer, Scrum Master, Product Owner, QA - Tester, Tech Lead, Software Analyst, Development Manager, Architect, Other
2. How many years of experience with Agile Software Development do you have?
   Options: 1 year or Less, 1 to 3 years, 4 to 7 years, 8 years or more
3. Which agile methodologies do you have experience with? (Select all that apply)
   Options: Scrum, Extreme Programming (XP), Lean, Crystal, Dynamic Systems Development Method (DSDM), Feature Driven Development (FDD), Scaled Agile Framework (SAFe), Large-Scale Scrum (LeSS), Others
4. Have you ever attended any training on any Agile Methodology?
   Options: Yes, No
5. How familiarized do you feel with agile methodologies?
   Options: Extremely familiarized, Very familiarized, Familiarized, Not so familiarized, not at all familiarized
6. How familiarized do you feel with Scaled Agile Framework (SAFe)?
   Options: Extremely familiarized, Very familiarized, Familiarized, Not so familiarized, not at all familiarized

7. How would you classify your degree of knowledge in each Agile Practice/Term?
   Options: Extremely confident, Very confident, Confident Not so confident, Not at all confident Practices and Terms: Iteration Planning, Retrospective, Iteration Review, Behavior Driven Development, Test Driven Development, Coding Standards, Estimation, Pair programming, Continuous Integration, Refactoring

8. Which means of communication do you prioritize to interact with other scrum teams, product owners or other teams involved in the project delivery?
   Options: (Select all that apply) E-mail, Phone, Skype Chat, Video Call, Face-to-face whenever possible

9. If the answer to the previous question was e-mail or Skype chat, what is the biggest impediment for having more phone, face-to-face or video calls communication?
   Options: (Select all that apply) Language barrier, Time zone constraints, Agenda conflicts (For example: not being able to find available time in the person's agenda to have a phone call), Others

10. How efficient would you classify communication via e-mail?
    Options: Extremely efficient, Very efficient, Somewhat efficient, Not so efficient, Not at all efficient

11. How efficient would you classify communication via Skype Chat?
    Options: Extremely efficient, Very efficient, Somewhat efficient, Not so efficient, Not at all efficient

12. How efficient would you classify communication via Phone Call?
    Options: Extremely efficient, Very efficient, Somewhat efficient, Not so efficient, Not at all efficient

13. How often do you discuss project related items or request feedback on features/stories developed with your Product Owner?
    Options: Almost on a daily basis, Once or twice per iteration, Every other iteration, Only during the PI Planning

14. How often do you have retrospective meetings with your scrum team?
    Options: Once per iteration, Once a month, Rarely, Never

15. Are your retrospective meetings resulting in actionable items to bring improvements? If your team never has retrospective meetings, please select 'Not Applicable'
    Options: Yes, No, Not applicable

16. How is your team planning each iteration's capacity according to the team's velocity?
    Options: We are usually over 100% capacity, We are usually at 100% capacity, We are usually around 80% capacity, We are usually below 80% capacity, We are not planning capacity according to team's velocity

17. How would you control/track the costs/budgets of an Agile project?
    Options: Through planned and defined budget to cover the life cycle of the project, Through initial budget to cover MVP and the remaining budget to be discussed depending on MVP results, Through incremental budget aligned in each phase, Not sure

18. In your opinion, what is/are the main challenge(s) of running an Agile development project with remote teams? This is a open ended question and response on this is optional.

References

1. Herbsleb, J.D., Moitra, D.: Global software development. IEEE Softw. **18**(2), 16–20 (2001). https://doi.org/10.1109/52.914732
2. Alqudah, M., Razali, R.: A review of scaling agile methods in large software development. Int. J. Adv. Sci. Eng. Inf. Technol. **6**(6), 828–837 (2016). https://doi.org/10.18517/ijaseit.6.6.1374
3. Paasivaara, M.: Adopting SAFe to scale agile in a globally distributed organization. In: 2017 IEEE 12th International Conference on Global Software Engineering (ICGSE), Buenos Aires, pp. 36–40 (2017). https://doi.org/10.1109/ICGSE.2017.15
4. Salinas, M.N., Neto, A.G., Emer, M.C.: Concerns and limitations in agile software development: a survey with Paraguayan companies. CoRR, abs/1710.01151 (2017)
5. Fitriani, W.R., Rahayu, P., Sensuse, D.I.: Challenges in agile software development: a systematic literature review. In: 2016 International Conference on Advanced Computer Science and Information Systems (ICACSIS), Malang, pp. 155–164 (2016). https://doi.org/10.1109/ICACSIS.2016.7872736
6. Hossain, E., Babar, M.A., Paik, H.: Using scrum in global software development: a systematic literature review. In: 2009 Fourth IEEE International Conference on Global Software Engineering, Limerick, pp. 175–184 (2009). https://doi.org/10.1109/ICGSE.2009.25
7. Nazir, N., Hasteer, N., Bansal, A.: A survey on agile practices in the Indian IT industry. In: 2016 6th International Conference - Cloud System and Big Data Engineering (Confluence), Noida, pp. 635–640 (2016). https://doi.org/10.1109/CONFLUENCE.2016.7508196

A Closing Paper From the Most Influential Researcher Over 10 Years of WBMA

Having Fun Doing Research on Agile Methods

Alfredo Goldman[1]([✉]), Thatiane de Oliveira Rosa[1,2], and Viviane A. Santos[3]

[1] University of São Paulo, São Paulo, SP, Brazil
{gold,thatiane}@ime.usp.br
[2] Federal Institute of Education, Science and Technology of Tocantins,
Paraíso do Tocantins, TO, Brazil
[3] Federal University of Pará, Tucuruí, PA, Brazil
vsantos@ufpa.br

Abstract. In this paper, we summarize the research done by the first author on Agile Methods in Brazil in a historical setting. In the beginning, Alfredo Goldman started as an enthusiast of Agile Methods, without pretending to become an agile advocate. However, as he perceived the importance of this new form of software development and in the belief of promoting a different way of looking at software engineering, naturally his contributions and achievements took him in this regard. We present Goldman's agile software development research topics, and their respective contributions. We had the hard task to summarize more than a decade of research in only one short text. We show the influence of his work within Agile Methods since 2001, not only on teaching, but also on the research field and on the Brazilian software development industry.

Keywords: Agile Methods advocate · Agility in Brazil · Historical perspective

1 Introduction

The genesis of this paper occurred in 2001 when we started teaching the course eXtreme Programming Laboratory at the University of São Paulo, Brazil. At that time, we were four professors seeking on how to improve the teaching of software engineering, using a very recent Agile Methodology to a few students. Since then the course has evolved, and after many years, agile methods became not only a part of our teaching but also one of our research topics.

Thanks to the support of Rebecca Wirfs-Brock, who had a close contact with several of our former students, we started to do a historical retrospective on the course evolution. Earlier this year we published a detailed report on the course history as an Experience Report on Agile 2019. A good history is worth telling.

Supported by CNPq under the grant 306518/2016-3. This study was financed in part by the Coordenação de Aperfeiçoamento de Pessoal de Nıvel Superior - Brasil (CAPES) - Finance Code 001.

ⓒ Springer Nature Switzerland AG 2019
P. Meirelles et al. (Eds.): WBMA 2019, CCIS 1106, pp. 147–164, 2019.
https://doi.org/10.1007/978-3-030-36701-5_12

The written report and the recorded video are available on the Agile Alliance web site[1].

Among the main findings of putting together all the events that happened on the last 18 years, we also figured out that the course was not only about teaching. We had collaboration with industry, actions to spread Agile Methods outside the University, and also students interested in conducting research on Agile Methods.

In this paper, we provide an overview of how the research on Agile Methods of the main author evolved over time. Showing several contributions and how they are related. Initially, the research is organized in a historical way, with a classical timeline. From it, we provide some insights about the different topics, and also show their main impacts.

This paper comes from a lot of cooperative work involving different people, after all, they became not only collaborators, but friends. It was a pleasure to share every moment during the development of the research topics.

In the next section we present an overview of the contributions, and their three main topics: Agility in Brazil, Agile Methods Education and Agile Methods Research. Then, we provide a quantitative and qualitative analysis. We then thank all the partners and conclude the paper.

2   Contributions

Our first paper on Agile Methods was a paper on the course itself, describing how to teach eXtreme Programming. It appeared in 2004, the professors involved on the course were the authors. Joseph Yoder also co-authored the paper, from the beginning he was our big supporter.

To provide a historical overview of the contributions, we first present the quantity of published papers in a timeline on Fig. 1. We also provide the keywords from each paper, organized by year.

We can observe that the first paper was published with a graduate student was in 2007. Observing the keywords, we can notice that at the beginning we were more interest in core aspects of Agile Methods, like metrics, tracking, informative workspaces and practices. The latter works are more focused on how to improve Agile Methods with concepts like Technical Debt, Organizational Learning and Group Psychology.

2.1   Agility in Brazil

In 2011, the Brazilian Symposium on Software Engineering (SBES 2011) had completed 25 years old in Brazil. This moment of celebration was ideal to reflect also on the progress of the agile movement in our country. Professor Alfredo along with his colleagues and students published a paper in this symposium presenting a brief overview of the genesis and evolution of the Agile Movement

---

[1] https://www.agilealliance.org/author/8035953.

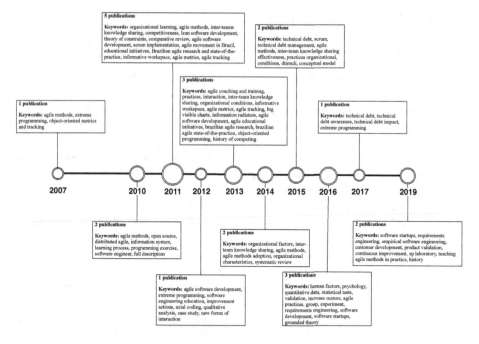

Fig. 1. Publications timeline

in Brazil [4]. This work has 23 citations and was then extended and published in the Journal of Brazilian Computer Society (JBCS) [12]. The paper has 56 citations and outlined the history of the national agile movement by presenting its first advocates in academia and industry.

In brief, it started in 1999, when Fabio Kon, a professor at the Computer Science Department of the Institute of Mathematics and Statistics (IME in Portuguese) at the University of São Paulo (USP), attended OOPSLA and by that time there was a great excitement around eXtreme Programming (XP). Then, in 2000, Sardinia (Italy) was the stage for the 1st International Conference on eXtreme Programming and Agile Processes in Software Engineering (XP' 2000). By that time, Fabio Kon and a few Brazilian software developers from academia and industry also got in touch with the international agile movement. Klaus Wuestefeld, a software developer working in the Brazilian software industry attended XP' 2000 and met key figures from the movement, such as Kent Beck, Alistair Cockburn, Martin Fowler, and others.

The first agile event in Brazil was Extreme Programming Brazil 2002 that was held in São Paulo. Similar initiatives were taken in other cities, such as Rio de Janeiro and Recife. In 2009, Agile Brazil was created to become the conference in Brazil joining scholars, professionals and companies around the agile methods theme. Other events were also created in Brazil, such as Agile Trends.

2.2   Agile Methods Education

We started to contribute to the agile methods education in 2001, when Kon returned from his post-doctoral leave in the USA, he started along with me (Prof. Alfredo Goldman), Prof. Paulo Silva e Silva, and Prof. Carlos Eduardo Ferreira a course on XP in which students would develop real software projects using all the XP practices rigorously [12]. It was called XP Laboratory and after some years, I (Alfredo) became responsible for this course.

The course teaches agile methods in practice, considering elements crucial for providing the student with real knowledge and experience. In 2010, the course went through changes [24]. We called it "the turning point" when we started to systematically apply agile methods to the course itself. It was possible when graduate students conducted empirical studies during the course as their master or Ph.D. studies. That made a great deal of improvements, since we started to apply practices, such as whole-class retrospectives in fishbowl format, lightning talks at lunchtime, rotation of team members across teams, brainwriting, coding dojos, Test Day and Refactoring Day, etc. In consequence, learning evolved and students started to continuously share and learn about technical knowledge, projects, agile methods, and skills.

After 18 years conducting this course, over 500 students taught to adopt Agile Methods, 15 empirical studies conducted, 84 projects executed and over 10 companies attended. We are proud to see our former students working on Agile Methods for companies in Brazil and all over the world, such as ThoughtWorks, DigitalOcean, IndustrialLogic, Amazon, Xero, Genios, among many others. XP Lab is consolidating in the world as a relevant educational initiative on Agile Methods [5].

In our perception, there is no closed formula to successfully teach Agile Methods in all contexts over and over again. We had to adapt to several different situations, and that is a good thing to point out. It is important to consider providing the environment and the support to the teams to work on real projects. Also, a good advice is to apply agile practices to improve the course itself and associate the learning environment not only for teaching, but also for researching. After all these years, the most important value of Agile Methods we have put into practice is continuous improvement, so we keep seeking ways to be better tomorrow than today.

2.3   Agile Methods Research

Considering the work of our master and Ph.D. students regarding agile methods, in Melo et al. [12], we described an overview of the status of Brazilian research on agile software development from 1999 to 2011. We searched in the Lattes Database. By that time, we identified 36 researchers on agile software development in that period, which advised 23 M.Sc. and Ph.D. students.

The studies fell into three thematic groups: introduction and adoption, use of tools and practices, and perceptions of agile methods. Experiences from the usage of agile software development can be identified mostly in commercial settings.

The results showed that agile methods research is growing in Brazil. More papers are being published, both in national and international conferences, also there are several Universities and research groups conducting research in different topics.

Now, we will describe in more details the research directed related to Professor Alfredo and his students.

Tracking Quality Metrics in Agile Projects. We know that the automated collection of source code metrics can help agile teams to understand better the software they are developing. The collected data can guide the adaptation of the adopted practices and favor the continuous improvement of the project. However, by 2007 this was not so straightforward.

Based on a bibliographic study, we selected eight of Object-Oriented (OO) metrics and analyzed their impact on five academic projects and two government projects. The aim was to observe and compare the evolution of these metrics in these projects and to evaluate how the different project context factors impacted the source code. The metrics adopted were: size and complexity metrics (LOC, v (G) and WMC), cohesion metric (LCOM), inheritance metrics (DIT, NOC) and coupling metrics (AC and EC). The results were published in 2007 in the proceedings of the International Conference on Extreme Programming and Agile Processes in Software Engineering [25].

The main contribution of this research was that the selected OO metrics may indicate the progress or lack of progress in adopting agile practices, such as testing and refactoring.

Investigating the Relationship Between Open Source and Agile Communities. The FLOSS Competence Center (CCSL) is located in the Institute of Mathematics and Statistics of the USP. Its aim is to understand the process of developing free software, and to contribute to its growth. In 2010, we investigated the relationship between the Agile community and the FLOSS community. The goal was to analyze if the strengths of both communities could be brought together to improve development in distributed environments with changing requirements. The results were published in the proceedings of the International Conference on Agile Software Development in 2010 [3].

We developed two questionnaires, one to the FLOSS community and the other to the Agile community respectively. We obtained 180 valid answers to the first form and 195 valid answers to the second one. During our research, we mapped team characteristics, communication channels and tools, and problem management. We realized that the FLOSS and Agile communities are slightly different, even if both communities identified the same issues and evaluated tools similarly. Both communities share the same issues regarding communication tools; expecting to simplify integration between developers and increase feedback frequency. Both FLOSS and Agile projects should have better results by using fast feedback communication channels such as face-to-face encounters or IRC channels instead of slower channels such as e-mails to communicate with the development team.

The main contribution of this research was to better understand similarities, strengths, and weaknesses of FLOSS and Agile communities to develop software in distributed environments with changing requirements.

Learning of Agile Practices. We were interested on better understanding how to teach Agile Practices, mainly based on a very popular technique at that time, Coding Dojos, which consists of providing a playground for developing code. A paper with the results was published in the proceedings of the International Conference on Agile Software Development in 2010 [2]. Its main aim was to investigate the use of Coding Dojo to learn agile practices such as pair programming, TDD, commits, retrospective and refactoring. The research was performed mainly in Brazil and had 91 collaborators. Different profiles from the collaborators were analyzed, including agile experts and beginners. Furthermore, the relationship between the Coding Dojo sessions and the acquired knowledge was also analyzed.

Based on the interviews, it was verified that Coding Dojo is a very effective technique for learning Agile practices, regardless of the experience. It was also noted that the less you know the more you will learn; and the more you participate in the sessions the more you will learn as well.

The contribution of this research was on validating Coding Dojos as an effective tool for learning.

Informative Workspace. Creating and maintaining an Informative Workspace (IW) is an important and challenging task in the context of agile projects, as it requires attention and balance from different aspects such as team adaptability, continuous reflection, workspace layout, human cognition, usability, and others. Furthermore, it can influence project communication dynamics, team behavior, and self-directed work.

In 2010, we realized that while there were some guidelines for creating and maintaining IW, there were few published empirical studies. In order to fill this gap, we developed two studies that explored procedures for creating and managing informative workspaces. The first study was published in 2011, in the proceedings of the Agile Conference [14]. The aim was to present a restricted set of heuristics to manage IW. The study was conducted in two phases, consisting of action research with suggestions, interviews and feedbacks for the elaboration of heuristics, and validation of them by the Brazilian agile community. We present a set of seven heuristics that can help professionals to create an effective informative workspace.

The second study is an extension of the first and was published in the proceedings of the International Conference on System Sciences [15] in 2013. It was carried out over two years and divided into four phases using action research, analysis of quantitative surveys, interviews and ground theory. The main goal was to understand how agile teams could optimize the use of informative workspace. As a result, we were able to identify WHY, HOW and WHEN the seven heuristics identified in the first study can be used.

We believe these two studies are a guide composed by concepts, patterns, heuristics, and valuable tips for creating and managing efficient IW.

From Manufacturing to the Agile Methods. In this research we aimed on better understanding the relationship on the agile methods derived from the manufacturing industry. At that time we found that researchers and practitioners were unaware of agile approaches for software development, and there was a lack of cumulative and reliable research in this context.

As a result, we published a paper in the Proceedings of the International Conference on Agile Software Development [8] in 2011, where we present a comparative review of agile methods derived from the manufacturing industry. We used six analytical perspectives of Abrahamsson et al. [1] for comparison purposes: project management support, life-cycle coverage, type of practical guidance, adaptability in current use, type of research objectives and the existence of empirical evidence. At the end of the review, we found that agile methods derived from the manufacturing industry cover various phases of the software development life-cycle. However, most of these methods do not provide adequate support for project management.

During the literature review, we found that there was only one systematic review of empirical studies on Agile Software Development. Furthermore, we noticed that most of the publications were not directly related to the topic of our research. As a result, the number of publications that needed to be analyzed was high. Thus, we needed to identify the most relevant publications to focus on. This motivated us to classify references based on our objective. Four categories were used to describe the status of empirical research on Lean Software Development and Constraint Theory: case study, empirical evidence, tools and practices, and conceptual study. Using this classification, we were able to map the number of publications on Lean Software Development and Constraint Theory per year for each category.

We consider that the main contribution of this research was a better understanding on the origin of Lean Software Development. Which allowed professionals to better perceive the properties of each agile method, and consequently choose the most appropriate method in a more grounded and systematic manner.

Organizational Learning and Knowledge Management. In 2011, we started to study in this area regarding agile software development (ASD). We had noted that agile methods strongly focused on empowering the project team in achieving its goals, but little attention was given to creating insights and experiences to the organizational level. So, we pointed out there is a challenge to overcome the barriers to scale the knowledge on the group level to the organizational level effectively [19]. We also studied the relationship between Scrum implementation and Organizational Learning process (Santos et al. 2011). We employed a qualitative research, involving key members from a company regarding content and services on the Internet in Brazil, key members from an academic project and an expert in agile methods implementation. Among the main findings, we highlight that the process of Organizational Learning could be verified through the individual members' learning and through the changes within the organization in management, people, process and technology. Beyond the relation established between Organizational Learning and Scrum implementation, this study contributes to academic and practical fields by the identification of changes occurred in type of knowledge valued, physical structure, promotion criteria, and individual dependence decrease when implementing Scrum. It is perceived that knowledge management, as a way of perpetuating the learning in the organization is still a challenge for agile software organizations.

In Santos et al. [23], we studied the role of agile coaches in agile methods implementation. An agile coach focuses on developing the potential of people and its application to obtain valuable results faster. This work analyzed the influence of the practices adopted by an agile consultant for enhancing overall interactions and knowledge sharing, such as Open Space and Lightning Talks sessions. We analyzed the influence of these practices in the organizational practices, as a way to foster organizational learning. We found significant associations between practices and purposes, and also crossed the level of adoption and barriers for adoption of the practices by company experience on agile methods. Results show that the participants recognize the positive impacts of the practices, but they are not sufficient to change the organizational practices. Few participants continue to adopt them in their organizations. Most of them report obstacles regarding organizational conditions, such as culture and top management/leadership support.

In [22], we employed a structural equation modeling and cross-table analysis, to analyze the influencing factors, such as organizational strategy, and communication flow and channels, regarding inter-team knowledge sharing (KS) effectiveness in agile environments. Within the surveyed companies, organizational strategy reflects on moderate commitment towards knowledge. KS practices are carried out to an acceptable standard. Extensive communication flow and the use of several channels denote that agile companies are also fostering interaction across teams. We found strong relationship between these factors and the companies' experience on agile methods. However, the companies still need to improve their strategy alignment to all organization levels. Thus, this study highlight the need consider these factors when implementing activities in this area.

After employing a deep qualitative research from 2011 to 2013, we offered a practical guidance on how to apply inter-team knowledge sharing [21]. We provided a pattern language to help agile software organizations to adopt practices for fostering interaction among agile teams in order to share knowledge across teams and create collective knowledge. For instance, Open Workspace helps to stimulate face-to-face conversations across teams. Rotation of Teams' Members is a practice about transferring of professionals to other teams in order to spread technical, methodological and management solutions in a sustainable way. Pair Programming among different teams are specially adopted to level technical knowledge throughout the company. Collective Meetings foster inter-team communication and alignment about company's projects and goals. Finally, Technical Presentations stimulate continuous learning and knowledge sharing behavior. The adoption of the pattern language is affected by forces, such as organizational culture, environment, and top management and leadership support. These forces need to be balanced to facilitate and/or reinforce the patterns.

As a result of the previous studies on this topic, we provided an understanding of the inter-team knowledge sharing activities in agile software development organizations and its effectiveness. We observed that the companies employ different work practices that allow knowledge sharing to occur across team boundaries. We raised a conceptual model that explained how effective knowledge sharing across agile teams depends on applying purposeful practices, along with organizational conditions and stimuli. This understanding suggested what is needed to take into account when considering this topic in the organization. Also, it presents opportunities for further studies in refining and extending the model to other organizational contexts. Inter-team knowledge sharing reflects the way agile software development organizations are coping with enterprise agility and the way they consider knowledge as a resource for competitiveness [20] (with 52 citations).

Agile Methods Industry Adoption. In 2012, we surveyed agile companies in Brazil, then we presented a report on the agile state-of-the-practice in the Brazilian IT industry involving agile methods adoption, practices, perceived benefits from adopting agile methods, main challenges, and relationships between companies experience, size, and Agile adoption factors and perceptions [13].

After that, we evaluated the impact of agile methods in industrial projects and discovered in which situations it is beneficial to apply such methods. In this paper [12], we presented an overview of the industry adoption. Agile methods were being widely adopted. The main reasons for this adoption were to accelerate time to market, to enhance the ability to manage changing priorities and to increase productivity.

The change in organizational culture appeared as an important element to facilitate agile adoption within companies. Also, the alignment between the companies values, mission, with the principles of the agile manifesto was the key aspect to facilitate the organizational cultural change. The understanding of the human factors and organizational change were main challenges to strengthen and sustain agile methods in industry. The initial champions of agile methods were developers and team leaders. In Brazil we had a bottom-up strategy, in contrast to the top-down strategy worldwide.

When we compared the results between Brazilian and worldwide surveys [30], we found very similar results about the benefits raised from implementing agile methods. But different practices were used based on companies' size and maturity on agile methods. Companies with more than five years of experience used practices such as refactoring, which is not the case for companies with less than three years of experience. A linear adoption of technical agile practices focused on enhancing software quality, such as TDD, refactoring, continuous integration and others, had been applied rigorously in companies more experienced in agile methods. However, management practices were the subset of agile practices undergoing major adjustments and even being abandoned, like the estimation techniques.

Agile Methods Adoption on Software Development. After more than a decade of the agile manifesto, we investigated the state of art of organizations adoption of agile methods. The aim was to find a correlation between the characteristics of organizations and the transition process adopted for the agile culture. We conducted a pilot systematic review, and the preliminary result was published in the proceedings of the Agile Conference, in 2014 [27].

To guide the implementation of the systematic review, we followed the recommendations of Kitchenham and Charters [9]. The main research question was: "Is it possible to report characteristics of organizations to the steps they take to adopt agile methods empirically?" We developed three secondary questions, which helped to answer the main question: 1. What are the existing generic ways to guide an organizational agile adoption? 2. What are the main steps taken by organizations that adopted agile methods empirically? 3. Is it possible to report steps from empiric agile adoptions in organizations to any of the existing generic ways?

The search was performed on the following search bases: ACM, Compendex, Elsevier, IEEE, SpringerLink, Agile Conference and XP Conference. Initially, 4062 studies were returned. After applying the inclusion and exclusion criteria, 96 publications remained for the qualitative analysis. This was the first learned lesson, there is plenty of published papers, it is difficult to find works related to the research content.

As a preliminary result, we have that there are at least 17 generic ways that can help organizations adopt agile methods. There are some success stories that signal that adopting Scrum is a good first step towards the agile journey. Furthermore, the organizational perspective can be considered a constraint for agile adoption. Although this study was published before completing the qualitative analysis stage of publications, it is possible to identify that its main contribution is some directions for organizations that wish to adopt the agile culture in their daily.

Managing Technical Debt in Agile Projects. The concept of technical debt emerged in 1992, and it is a metaphor for immature, incomplete or inadequate software artifacts. These debts are incurred in order to meet budget or schedule constraints imposed by the reality of business. With this, having technical debts is inevitable. Therefore, it is useless to try to eliminate them entirely, but it is essential to manage them.

Two studies that analyzes the relationship between Technical debt and Agile Methods were made. The first research was published in the proceedings of the Agile Conference [17] in 2015. This research aimed to evaluate the technical debt management framework proposed by Seaman and Guo [26] in a real software development environment using Scrum.

At the time, we found that managing technical debt on projects using Scrum was difficult because of the following reasons: It is not clear who is responsible for minimizing technical debt; the product owner often does not understand the need and benefits of reducing technical debt; and issues and goals related to technical debt were neither structured nor documented.

The methodology adopted for this experiment was action research, and two projects were selected. The following guidelines were adopted to select the candidate projects: ongoing projects with frequent change requests; projects using Scrum for management; projects with evidence of unmanaged technical debt.

The experiment results are as follows. After some adjustments, the teams of both projects recognized that the approach proposed to manage technical debt was viable. We reduced the number of proposed metrics to two because of time constraints and ease of use. The metrics are: Principal and the Current Amount of Interest. Consequently, decision-making was improved by considering debts that really needed to be paid early. During the first research phase, debt identification was improved when all Scrum roles participated. Furthermore, both measurement and decision making were improved when the team was responsible for these phases. The Product Owner in both companies understood the importance of monitoring and prioritizing technical debt during the development cycle. After conducting the study, both teams concluded that they would continue to support and use the resulting approach.

The main contribution of this research was to provide real experience and improvements to software teams that use Scrum, which may adopt the technical debt management framework proposed by Seaman and Guo [26].

The second research was published in 2017 where we conducted an empirical study in an academic environment. In this study, we identified the effects of technical debt awareness, such as the influence on team behavior.

Drawing on Methods and Theories from Psychology. The first paper [6] we published that drew directly on the psychology research field was to shortly investigate the use of psychometrics in software engineering research. At the time, survey research was common in software engineering research, but the statistical validation techniques created in psychological test theory were not. Since this paper was published in 2016, the focus on psychometrics in software engineering has increased and a very recent book chapter focuses on many of these aspects [31]. There is, however, still a need to apply the methods we suggested on a larger scale, as argued by Wagner et al. [31].

The second paper [7] drew on both novel theory from psychology in the software engineering context, and showed an example of a more classic experiment with in intervention and a control group. The theory used was a social-psychological theory on team development from a group dynamics perspective. We drew on the theory by Wheelan [32]. The theory comprises four different developmental stages of all human small groups trying to reach a common goal. We randomly divided seven student groups from the XP course at USP into an experimental group and a control group and trained the experimental group in group dynamics for 1.5 h. We also measured their agile practices maturity by using the survey created by So and Scholl [28]. While we obtained great feedback from the students on the importance of team maturity, we did not see a significant effect in our repeated measurements data analysis.

We speculated that 1.5 h of training was too little to push the team forward in its psychological development, or that there are other confounding factors we would have needed to take into account. We also state that the sample might be too small and that we need a larger dataset to find a small effect.

Even if we could not draw many conclusions on from this paper, we still showed an example of how to conduct an analyze classical experiment in human factors research in software engineering that draw on both theories and statistical methods from psychology. We also reported that we saw the importance of looking at teams as a unit of analysis more, which we are happy to say has become more prominent in software engineering research lately [16].

Software Startups. Software startups are companies that develop innovative, software-intensive products or services [29] in a context characterized by a general lack of resources, high reactiveness and flexibility, intense time-pressure, uncertain conditions, and fast growth [18]. Although agile methodologies have been seen as a natural approach to be used in software development in these organizations, some challenges may arise. For instance, customer feedback, one of the pillars of agile, is hindered since, in the beginning, there are no customers for an innovative product. In an initial effort to better understand this concept and since, by the beginning of the research, there were few studies on software engineering practices in startups and none focused on requirements engineering [18], we decided to focus on this aspect that is the boundary between business and software development. Therefore, we conducted a grounded theory study to understand how requirements engineering activities are carried out in software startups. The research was conceived in cycles consisted of interviews with founders and employees of software startups and data analysis based on open and axial coding. In the first cycle, we performed 9 interviews and inductively developed a model. These preliminary results were presented in the *2nd International Workshop on Software Startups* [10]. Until theoretical saturation was reached, we performed other two cycles, totalizing 17 interviews with 23 people involved that had experience with more than 30 startups. The final results were published in the *Information and Software Technology* journal [11].

Our findings show that software startups do not follow a single specific set of practices for requirements engineering, instead they follow a custom process built based on set of influences: founders, software development manager, developers, business model, market, and ecosystem. Besides that, practices are similar to those of agile methodologies with some differences regarding the lack of a customer to have feedback on. A common practice to tackle this problem is the figure of a product team. An internal multi-disciplinary team (or single person) to think about the product and act as a proxy of possible customers.

During the period in which we developed this study, the software startup research flourished. The initial paper has been cited in different empirical studies about software development, in general, and requirements engineering, in specific, in software startups. The research also offered one of the first empirical studies on software startups in Brazil. Finally, the study is the cornerstone of Melegati's next research: to improve the use of continuous experimentation, a new trend in agile software development, in software startups. The model developed provides the set of factors that should be analyzed and acted upon to improve the usage of this new agile practices in this context.

Effects of Technical Debt Awareness: A Classroom Study. The aim of this research was to observe the effects of Technical Debt awareness in teams in an academic setting. For this we followed the Extreme Programming Laboratory (XP Lab) at the University of São Paulo. This study aimed to answer the following research question (RQ): What was the impact on the team when Technical Debt was explicitly considered? The study was applied in two editions of XP Lab. Four teams were followed in the 2013 edition and five teams in the 2014 edition.

We conducted the study and collected data through questionnaires and interviews, and analyzed the source code of the projects with Sonar Qube and Code Climate tools to identify the impact on the teams that explicitly considered Technical Debt (TD). The teams had some similar views on the importance and benefits of making TD explicit. A significant finding is that the teams considered it very helpful because they could see the whole landscape of the software quality (they knew which part of the software had immature code). They also emphasized that it was very useful to have a board where every day they could see the health of the code. Before becoming aware of TD, the team members reported that they sometimes incurred TD but never remembered to go back and correct it. But after considering TD, they thought about the necessity of incurring TD and often decided against it. Also, they could see the TD list and so they did not forget the TD items that needed to be addressed. They discussed more about how to implement the tasks, also they talked more about the problems of the software because they had the list of the TDs visible. This process of thinking about incurring or not TD, discussing about it and reviewing the TD during the project can create a culture focused on improving the software quality. In addition, in this study we explored some ways of identifying and monitoring TD. Our research participants found some form of a TD board very useful for documenting TD, making it visible, and adjusting both the TD board and their behavior accordingly. By using the TD board, they always know the list of software deficiencies so have a constant reminder of how to organize their work and improve the software. As a complementary aid, they may use tools to help them to identify and monitor TD occurrence. However, it is important to highlight that tool reports provide a static analysis of the software quality and some TD item could not be identified using static metrics.

The results of this study could motivate teams to consider TD further, to help developers convince leaders and directors, the decision makers, to start considering TD. These approaches used by the XP Lab teams, such as boards, cards and tools can help teams in companies to deal with TD. In addition, they could define the list of TD items that are crucial to the project but hard to identify with the tools. As a result they can define a strategy to deal with the TD over time. As communication in the team was improved, all team members thought more about quality, not just specific members. The "agile" culture of the teams improved and in addition, the team believed that it was easier to show the impact of the TD level to clients, showing that it is possible to invest some time to improve the quality. The main results emphasize the Extreme Programming values and helped the teams to support values such as communication at all levels, courage to change and feedback to continuously improve the software.

The main outcome of both studies on TD was to allow to improve the Agile Methods context of the teams, using an additional mindset which would improve the development process.

3   Quantitative and Qualitative Analysis

In the Fig. 2 we can check the number of citations on August 2019 on Google Scholar for each of the papers discussed above. Looking in a retrospective way, we do not have any reasonable explanation on why some papers are cited much more that others. A more careful analysis on the citations would be needed to clarify this differences.

Fig. 2. Citations number per publication

We also tried to understand the citation pattern for the Top 5 most cited papers (Fig. 3). Again there is no evident pattern. The only clear point is that 2017 was a good year to be cited, but without any clear reason.

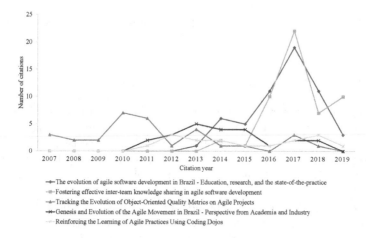

Fig. 3. Evolution of citations number - Top 5

For the qualitative analysis we observed how the several papers were cited, looking for top conferences like ICSE and top journals like Empirical Software

Table 1. Qualitative analysis

Paper	Cited in
Fostering effective inter-team knowledge sharing in agile software development	Journal of Systems and Software in 2016
Agile Methods Adoption on Software Development: A Pilot Review	Empirical Software Engineering in 2017
Managing Technical Debt in Software Projects Using Scrum: An Action Research	Journal of Systems and Software in 2017
The evolution of agile software development in Brazil - Education, research, and the state-of-the-practice	ICSE in 2017; Information and Software Technology in 2017 and 2018
Trying to Increase the Mature Use of Agile Practices by Group Development Psychology Training - An Experiment	ICSE-SEIP in 2018
Requirements engineering in software startups: A grounded theory approach	ICSE in 2018; IEEE Software in 2018 and 2019; Empirical Software Engineering in 2019; IEEE Transactions on Software Engineering in 2019; Information and Software Technology in 2019
A model of requirements engineering in software startups	Information and Software Technology in 2019

Engineering, Transactions in Software Engineering, IEEE Software, Information ad Software Technology and Journal of Systems and Software. The main citations are depicted on Table 1.

In summary, seven papers were cited. They were written in English, and were published both in conferences and journals. The most cited one is very recent, however, it studies a very popular subject. Requirements analysis for software startups.

4   Conclusions

After taking the time to put together the experiences learned on this long journey, we have some takeaways. In the beginning, the research on Agile Methods was more focused on small experiments, and more simple settings. Now, it is primordial to perform validations on real environments, using both qualitative and quantitative methods combined with modern techniques of Empirical Software Engineering.

Another takeaway is related to broadening the research, not only to consider the developers themselves, but also the developers' context, the stakeholders and their interactions. Software developments depends on many more factors than just practices, and processes, the context itself has to be taken into account.

Finally, after all these years teaching, spreading and doing research on Agile Methods, we can affirm that we are happy with the transformation. From the start where the Agile Manifesto was known for few programmers to now, were Agile became mainstream. Thanks, mainly to the Agile Methods, today to be Agile has become the norm. But, we always have to take the developers side into account, remembering that there are technical skills that are needed, and in our opinion, this is the next challenge to be solved. How to couple the current Agile mindset with the developers and their needs. The solution encompasses a tight collaboration among three main pillars: Education, Research and Practice.

There is much work to be done researching on Agile Methods, join us.

Acknowledgments. One of the main take-outs of this journey was to deeply understand that research is not an activity to be done alone. So, we have to thank all the people involved on the papers cited. So, chronologically, we want to thank: Fabio Kon, Paulo Silva e Silva, Carlos Ferreira, Joe Yoder, Danilo Sato, Hugo Corbucci Mariana Bravo, Renan de Melo Oliveira, Cláudia Melo, Eduardo Katayama, Viviane Santos, Caio Silva, Frederico Oliveira, Graziela Tonin, Jorge Melegati, Lucas Gren, Diogo Pina, Luis Gustavo Araujo Rodriguez.

References

1. Abrahamsson, P., Oza, N., Siponen, M.T.: Agile software development methods: a comparative review[1]. In: Dingsøyr, T., Dybå, T., Moe, N. (eds.) Agile software development, pp. 31–59. Springer, Heidelberg (2010). https://doi.org/10.1007/978-3-642-12575-1_3

2. Bravo, M., Goldman, A.: Reinforcing the learning of agile practices using coding *Dojos*. In: Sillitti, A., Martin, A., Wang, X., Whitworth, E. (eds.) XP 2010. LNBIP, vol. 48, pp. 379–380. Springer, Heidelberg (2010). https://doi.org/10.1007/978-3-642-13054-0_41

3. Corbucci, H., Goldman, A.: Open source and agile methods: two worlds closer than it seems. In: Sillitti, A., Martin, A., Wang, X., Whitworth, E. (eds.) XP 2010. LNBIP, vol. 48, pp. 383–384. Springer, Heidelberg (2010). https://doi.org/10.1007/978-3-642-13054-0_43

4. Corbucci, H., Goldman, A., Katayama, E., Kon, F., Melo, C., Santos, V.: Genesis and evolution of the agile movement in Brazil-perspective from academia and industry. In: 2011 25th Brazilian Symposium on Software Engineering, pp. 98–107. IEEE (2011)

5. Goldman, A., Santos, V.A.: Sharing techniques to continuously improve the XP laboratory. In: 2019 Agile Conference (2019)

6. Gren, L., Goldman, A.: Useful statistical methods for human factors research in software engineering: a discussion on validation with quantitative data. In: Proceedings of the 9th International Workshop on Cooperative and Human Aspects of Software Engineering, pp. 121–124. ACM (2016)

7. Gren, L., Goldman, A.: Trying to increase the mature use of agile practices by group development psychology training-an experiment. arXiv preprint arXiv:1904.02466 (2019)

8. Katayama, E.T., Goldman, A.: From manufacture to software development: a comparative review. In: Sillitti, A., Hazzan, O., Bache, E., Albaladejo, X. (eds.) XP 2011. LNBIP, vol. 77, pp. 88–101. Springer, Heidelberg (2011). https://doi.org/10.1007/978-3-642-20677-1_7

9. Kitchenham, B., Charters, S.: Guidelines for performing systematic literature reviews in software engineering (2007)

10. Melegati, J., Goldman, A.: Requirements engineering in software startups: a grounded theory approach. In: 2nd International Workshop on Software Startups (2016)

11. Melegati, J., Goldman, A., Kon, F., Wang, X.: A model of requirements engineering in software startups. Inf. Softw. Technol. **109**(July 2018), 92–107 (2019). https://doi.org/10.1016/j.infsof.2019.02.001

12. Melo, C.O., et al.: The evolution of agile software development in Brazil. J. Braz. Comput. Soc. **19**(4), 523 (2013)

13. Melo, C.d.O., Santos, V.A., Corbucci, H., Katayama, E., Goldman, A., Kon, F.: Métodos ágeis no brasil: estado da prática em time e organizações (2012)

14. de Melo Oliveira, R., Goldman, A.: How to build an informative workspace? an experience using data collection and feedback. In: 2011 Agile Conference, pp. 143–146. IEEE (2011)

15. de Melo Oliveira, R., Goldman, A., Melo, C.O.: Designing and managing agile informative workspaces: discovering and exploring patterns. In: 2013 46th Hawaii International Conference on System Sciences, pp. 4790–4799. IEEE (2013)

16. Moe, N.B., Stray, V., Hoda, R.: Trends and updated research agenda for autonomous agile teams: a summary of the second international workshop at XP2019. In: Hoda, R. (ed.) XP 2019. LNBIP, vol. 364, pp. 13–19. Springer, Cham (2019). https://doi.org/10.1007/978-3-030-30126-2_2

17. Oliveira, F., Goldman, A., Santos, V.: Managing technical debt in software projects using scrum: an action research. In: 2015 Agile Conference, pp. 50–59. IEEE (2015)

18. Paternoster, N., Giardino, C., Unterkalmsteiner, M., Gorschek, T., Abrahamsson, P.: Software development in startup companies: a systematic mapping study. Inf. Softw. Technol. **56**(10), 1200–1218 (2014)
19. Santos, V., Goldman, A.: An approach on applying organizational learning in agile software organizations. In: Sillitti, A., Hazzan, O., Bache, E., Albaladejo, X. (eds.) XP 2011. LNBIP, vol. 77, pp. 324–325. Springer, Heidelberg (2011). https://doi. org/10.1007/978-3-642-20677-1_27
20. Santos, V., Goldman, A., De Souza, C.R.: Fostering effective inter-team knowledge sharing in agile software development. Empir. Softw. Eng. **20**(4), 1006–1051 (2015)
21. Santos, V., Goldman, A., Guerra, E., De Souza, C., Sharp, H.: A pattern language for inter-team knowledge sharing in agile software development. In: Proceedings of the 20th Conference on Pattern Languages of Programs, p. 20. The Hillside Group (2013)
22. Santos, V., Goldman, A., Martins, D., Cortés, M., et al.: The influence of organizational factors on inter-team knowledge sharing effectiveness in agile environments. In: 2014 47th Hawaii International Conference on System Sciences, pp. 4729–4738. IEEE (2014)
23. Santos, V., Goldman, A., Roriz Filho, H.: The influence of practices adopted by agile coaching and training to foster interaction and knowledge sharing in organizational practices. In: 2013 46th Hawaii International Conference on System Sciences, pp. 4852–4861. IEEE (2013)
24. Santos, V.A., Goldman, A., Santos, C.D.: Uncovering steady advances for an extreme programming course. CLEI Electron. J. **15**(1), 2–2 (2012)
25. Sato, D., Goldman, A., Kon, F.: Tracking the evolution of object-oriented quality metrics on agile projects. In: Concas, G., Damiani, E., Scotto, M., Succi, G. (eds.) XP 2007. LNCS, vol. 4536, pp. 84–92. Springer, Heidelberg (2007). https://doi. org/10.1007/978-3-540-73101-6_12
26. Seaman, C., Guo, Y.: Measuring and monitoring technical debt. In: Advances in Computers, vol. 82, pp. 25–46. Elsevier (2011)
27. Silva, C.C., Goldman, A.: Agile methods adoption on software development: a pilot review. In: 2014 Agile Conference, pp. 64–65. IEEE (2014)
28. So, C., Scholl, W.: Perceptive agile measurement: new instruments for quantitative studies in the pursuit of the social-psychological effect of agile practices. In: Abrahamsson, P., Marchesi, M., Maurer, F. (eds.) XP 2009. LNBIP, vol. 31, pp. 83–93. Springer, Heidelberg (2009). https://doi.org/10.1007/978-3-642-01853-4_11
29. Unterkalmsteiner, M., et al.: Software startups - a research agenda. e-Informatica Softw. Eng. J. **10**(1), 1–28 (2016)
30. VersionOne: 5th annual state of agile development survey. Technical report, VersionOne (2010)
31. Wagner, S., Mendez, D., Felderer, M., Graziotin, D., Kalinowski, M.: Challenges in survey research. arXiv preprint arXiv:1908.05899 (2019)
32. Wheelan, S.A., Hochberger, J.M.: Validation studies of the group development questionnaire. Small group Res. **27**(1), 143–170 (1996)

Author Index

Printed in the United States
By Bookmasters